What a blessing this book is to all who are grieving the loss of a loved one or pondering their own passing. Jane Amelia Smith's own experience of grief led her on a quest to understand what lies on the other side of the thin line between life and death. Within *Rx for Grief: Hope through God's Truth,* she shares her travel journal with readers, so to speak. After presenting concise summaries of the major world religions' beliefs and teachings on the afterlife, Jane turns to a fascinating examination of near death experiences (NDEs) and what they can tell us about life beyond death. I found the sections on quantum physics gripping and believe the author has made a compelling case for the compatibility of new advances in physics and the Christian belief in the afterlife.

Scott Philip Stewart, Ph.D.

Jane Amelia Smith has written a wonderfully comprehensive, pleasing explanation of the gospel. Compelled by the death of four very significant loved ones, and the inescapable reality that life ends in death, Jane searched, studied, and re-discovered the hope and comfort found in the gospel. Having given studious attention to multiple resources, she has provided honest, fair observations and drawn conclusive evidence that builds to defeat doubt. This is so rightly written for the inquisitive skeptic who may be curious enough to consider the possibility of life after death, the existence of God, and the person of Jesus Christ. I picked up this book and read it straight through, and became increasingly excited as Jane provided more and more substance and greater assurance for her proclamation of the gospel. I am so eager to share *Rx for Grief: Hope through God's Truth* with an audience awaiting a reason to believe!

CH (COL) Jim Park, USAR, (Ret.)
Institute Chaplain (Ret.)
Virginia Military Institute

This book offers a fresh look into the concept of death, grief, and the journey toward faith. Whether you are an atheist, someone on the fence about faith, or someone who wants to be ready with an answer for their faith, this book pulls together several lines of thought from various religions, science, and theology into a thoughtful defense of the Christian faith. *Rx for Grief: Hope through God's Truth* is an encouraging reminder that earthly death is not the end.

Patricia V. Cunningham, Ph.D. in Immunology
UC Berkeley; Colson Fellow

FOR GRIEF

Hope through God's Truth

BY

JANE AMELIA SMITH

Deep River BOOKS

ISBN–13: 9781632695505
Library of Congress Control Number: 2020915162

Printed in the USA

Cover design by Robin Black, Inspirio Design

Other Books Written by the Author

Finding Amelia

A Soul for Amicus

Dedication

In loving memory of
My parents: Fred and Amelia Budenbender
My late husband: Richard W. Smith
My best friend: Connie Orcutt Block

Special thanks to . . .

My husband, Roger D. Goughnour, who brought love back into my life, and later shared his expertise in Scripture interpretation to assist in the writing of this book.

My dear friends, Patricia V. Cunningham, Jim Park, Anne and Chris Thulin, for taking the time from their busy lives to read the manuscript for this book, ultimately providing for valuable feedback.

My independent editor, Scott Philip Stewart, PhD, for his meticulous edit of my manuscript: Christian Author Services, www.ChristianBookEditor.com, P.O. Box 870572, Stone Mountain, GA 30087.

My publisher, Andy Carmichael, Deep River Books, and his talented staff, for transforming my words into the book I had envisioned it to be.

All the wise and insightful authors referenced within this book, whose faith journey became my own.

My personal Savior, Jesus Christ, who has tenaciously held on to me throughout the peaks and valleys of my life.

Contents

Disclaimer

This book was written for the sole purpose of assuring those grieving for loved ones or facing their own imminent demise that God is true to His word, and those who live in Him will have everlasting life. This book in no way condones taking one's own precious life in suicide so as to escape the less than perfect world we all live in. Everything was meant to happen in God's time alone, both our living and our dying, and only in God is either activity worthwhile. Please refer to Chapter 10, "Full Circle," to learn more about this desperate act and its tragic consequences.

Submit yourselves therefore to God. Resist the devil, and he will flee from you. (James 4:7, KJV)

Introduction

*W*e all live with death every day of our lives. It matters little the number of years we have lived, whether we are rich or poor, plain or beautiful, smart or dull, godly or ungodly; the shadow of death looms over us. When death beckons us we are obliged to go. But *where* do we go, if indeed we go anywhere? Is death truly the end of all we are—not merely the physical matter that holds us together but our very essence, our consciousness, as well? Though a person's belief system may be firmly in place, it is unlikely that any one of us will find answers to all of our questions over a lifetime.

The purpose of this book is not to debate those religious tenets available to us, nor is it a presumptuous attempt to fill in all of the blanks pertaining to death. Rather, in this book I present comparative belief systems, as well as scientific advances that help broaden our perspective as to what possibly happens during the dying process and thereafter. I wrote this book for the realist who understands the temporal nature of all life as we know it. I hope the words that follow will bring a beacon of comfort to those who have lost a loved one or who await their own inevitable demise.

Finally, this is a book for the adventurer, for life and death as we know it is the ultimate adventure—one that entices many to forge a clearer understanding as to where we might be headed. I invite you to share in my journey; if you like, turn the page and let's begin!

O teach me, Lord, that I may teach
The precious things Thou dost impart;
And wing my words that they may reach
The hidden depths of many a heart.

Francis R. Havergal, 1872

"I Love You" . . . Truly

These things will last forever—faith, hope, and love—and the greatest of these is love. (1 Corinthians 13:13)

I cannot help but wonder if most of us really understand the commitment and feeling that were intended to be associated with the words "I love you." Do any of us really understand what we are committing to when we say or write those words, or have they been reduced to an empty platitude?

When faced with the barrage of headlines reporting on the pandemic violence within families, I cannot help but believe this is indeed the case. The United States alone has between 960,000 and 3,000,000 reported cases of domestic violence yearly. Its victims include not only women but children and men as well.

In addition, 40 to 50 percent of marriages within the United States end in divorce. Interestingly, the divorce rate has decreased over the years, primarily due to the fact that people are marrying later or avoiding marriage entirely in favor of less binding relationships. Apparently even the fear of losing at love can be a deterrent to the commitment of a marriage relationship.

It is true that love is not for the faint of heart, and the odds are good that at some point, due to any number of possibilities—including losing a loved one through death—we will be hurt because we chose to love. The love referred to in this book is not the distorted version often fabricated by narcissistic and ill-equipped individuals, where self is always the main focus. Narcissists are able to acknowledge your existence only if you serve to fulfill a personal need; they are devoid of empathy and believe that the rules do not apply to them. The selfish person, though self-centered, still has empathy as well as moral boundaries. Neither, however, is capable of loving themselves or others in the way the Lord intended.[1]

We will be able to love others only if we love and respect ourselves. The Bible recognizes that we must love ourselves first, and it instructs us, "Love your neighbor as yourself" (Mark 12:31).

Deviant interpersonal relationships are often mislabeled as love: *sadomasochism* between consenting adults either in or out of marriage; *smother love* directed at our children; *living vicariously* through one's offspring; as well as any instance in which emotional and/or physical *abuse or neglect* are practiced. True love flows from the Holy Spirit within us and through us and brings blessings to everyone we encounter. This is the love for which we were created, the love we are unable to live without.

Love generated through the Holy Spirit works within every form of human love we might experience, be it the love between sweethearts, between husbands and wives, parents and children, friends and neighbors, strangers, and most certainly our love for God. Within this context, love has everything to do with everything, and whatever hurt or suffering comes as a consequence of loving to this extent is well worth it.

Forms of Love

Over the ages songs, sonnets, and Christian hymns have expounded upon both the virtues and the pitfalls of love. When we listen to the lyrics of popular songs or Christian hymns, we can easily decipher the distinct love scenarios within each genre of music. The forms of love recognized in psychiatry and other mental health disciplines include:

- *eros*, sexual or passionate love;
- *philia*, friendship or good will;
- *storge*, familial love between parents and children;
- *agape*, universal love for strangers, nature, or God;
- *ludus*, playful or uncommitted love;

- *pragma*, practical love founded on reason or duty of one's long-term interests; and

- *philautia*, self-love, which can be healthy or unhealthy.[2]

The Bible speaks of four of the above types of love: *eros*, *storge*, *philia*, and a*gape* love.[3] Renowned social psychologist, psychoanalyst, and humanist Dr. Erich Fromm affirms what the Bible has told us for millennia: love is the answer to the problem of human existence. It is little wonder that individuals who have returned from near-death experiences (NDEs) commonly focus on the importance of loving one another. In his book *The Art of Loving,* Dr. Fromm states:

> Love is an active power in man; a power which breaks through the walls which separate man from his fellowmen, which unites him with others, love makes him overcome the sense of isolation and separateness, yet it permits him to be himself, to retain his integrity.[4]

The separateness and aloneness that we humans so often feel go well beyond our personal relationships with one another; they are a reflection of our individual separation from God our Maker. Only through inviting God into our lives will we be empowered to love the way in which He intended, instead of settling for the numerous forms of counterfeit love generated through the desperation of man.

So what exactly is this thing called love, and is it necessarily elusive and unobtainable? Within Western culture the word "love" immediately brings to mind romantic love, or *eros*. If you are fortunate enough to have experienced a Valentine love, you understand the feeling of euphoria expressed within love songs. As wonderful as this form of love can be, it must either flower into a more mature love, capable of surviving the test of time, or it is sure to die. That is not to say that a mature love is without romance, but romantic love must evolve into something much deeper and more fulfilling than what was there at its inception.

Love Is Active

Love is always an active endeavor, and lovers can never rest upon their laurels. In order to sustain any love relationship (except the love between young children and parents), those involved in the relationship must focus upon giving rather than receiving love. Even so, if a love relationship is truly generated through the Holy Spirit, neither party will lose sight of his/her own integrity or the integrity of his/her loved one. In this regard, Fromm writes, "What is given in love is the most precious attribute any human being has, one gives of themselves, their very life is given to the other."[5]

You may be asking yourself: How is love of this nature achieved? For at least two thousand years, Jesus Christ, throughout the New Testament of the Bible, has given us the recipe for loving God, ourselves, and one another.

Fromm concurs with much that is written in both the Old and New Testaments pertaining to the art of loving (with the exception as to where that love stems from—either man or God). To sum up Dr. Fromm's directives for achieving fulfilling love relationships, he gives us these primary ingredients for success:

> First a clear understanding of what love is and what it is not, love is not only a feeling but a commitment as well. Next, the art of loving must be practiced every day, and lastly we must make loving others the primary concern within our lives.[6]

Basic elements in any loving relationship must include *care, responsibility, respect,* and *knowledge.* In addition, only a *rational faith,* in ourselves as well as others, will allow us the courage required to risk loving someone else.[7]

Jesus Christ risked everything for humankind as He hung in agony on a cross, leading to His death and resurrection so that we might be cleansed of our sins and resurrected through Him to eternal life with God our Father. This is and always will be the best example of selfless love the world will ever know. And though in literal terms we probably will not be asked to die on a cross, we are meant to emulate Jesus' love toward others in our daily lives. The Bible gives us a clear picture of what real love looks like:

> Love is patient, love is kind. It does not envy, it does not boast, it is not proud. It does not

dishonor others, it is not self-seeking, it is not easily angered, and it keeps no record of wrongs. Love does not delight in evil but rejoices with the truth. It always protects, always trusts, always hopes, and always perseveres. Love never fails. (1 Corinthians 13:4–8, NIV)

The human race has always thirsted after a deep and abiding love—but except for brief moments in history and in our own lives, it continues to elude us. Since the beginning of time our struggle to achieve a universal love on planet Earth has continued to flounder within many pointless twists and turns. From the humanist standpoint, Fromm suggests that "the power of love exists in every human being, all that is required is the establishment of an environment conducive to a humanitarian ideology," or, from his standpoint, a socialistic form of government.[8] Yet to date, every form of government implemented through the mind and hand of man—be it a monarchical system, socialism, communism, or capitalism—has failed to produce a world of brotherly love.

God Himself provided for such a society in the Garden of Eden, where all but two human beings were sustained by the God of the universe. God met Adam and Eve's every need. They neither strived nor worried, yet they failed in their love for God and one another. It did not take long before pride and disobedience raised their ugly heads, causing all of creation to lose so much more than merely a free lunch.

Mankind more often than not forgets that although humans were created beautiful in God's own image, we are neither God—nor will we ever be as such. If humankind continues on the slippery slope of rejecting God, it will succeed in nothing more than cutting itself free from the vine, resulting in spiritual death. Should that come to pass, the Holy Spirit will withdraw from humankind, leaving human sinful nature to rein unbridled. Without the Holy Spirit within and among us, God's love can no longer be manifested through any of us. Consequently no government on earth through man alone will succeed in ushering in that utopia so many of us dream of. Without God Almighty at the helm, there will never be peace on planet Earth.

Therefore, during the short time we are here—and even in the face of death and grieving—our time will be well spent only if we emulate that same love Jesus Christ first showed us. Only through the Holy Spirit's presence within us will we ever come close to being able to express a love of this caliber. If you believe you are not there yet—and none of us is there yet, it might be best to continue to pray in good faith that God will deliver you from yourself. Then and only then will you be able to take your own small steps for the one and only amazing Lord God.

A Personal Note

I wasn't ready to write a book of this nature earlier in my life. My two previous books were Christian fiction, and it was not necessary for me to reveal anything of my personal life as I am about to do in this book. Writing has always been a wonderful release for me, now more so than ever before. In this book I felt it necessary to share my own experiences of life, death, grieving, and life once again, as you may be dealing with many of the same issues right now. If you are a believer in Jesus Christ you already know what a comfort He is when you are grieving the loss of a loved one through death or even estrangement.

If by chance you are not a believer, I ask you to search harder, read more—both the Bible and those books pertaining to current scientific revelations (as I discuss briefly in the following chapters). I am hopeful that as you do, someday you may also be able to proclaim, as Corrie ten Boom did, "Never be afraid to trust an unknown future to a known God."[9]

Chapter 2

Journey by Design

> "For I know the plans I have for you," says the LORD. "They are plans for good and not for disaster, to give you a future and hope." (Jeremiah 29:11)

*D*o you believe that God has a plan for your life? I believe that He does, just as He has a plan for my life. This belief has so overtly played out in my own life that I am compelled to share some of my story with you.

My Own Story

Again, I couldn't have written this book even a decade earlier. In the relatively short span of fifteen years, my faith journey has taken me well beyond where I had been earlier in my life. In a short period of time I lost both my loving parents to illness and old age, my closest college friend to cancer—and then, two months later experienced the tragic, unexpected death of my husband in an accident. I will spare you the details of how devastated and alone I felt, even though I had been raised in the Christian faith and believed in life beyond the grave.

You see, I was one of those many Christians who, if surveyed, would have quickly checked the box stating I was a Christian, only to go my merry way with little thought as to what impact that acknowledgment should have upon every decision I made for myself in this life. Now, years beyond the passing of the four people I loved most in this world, I continue to discover the impact that each death has made upon me and my faith in God.

When my parents died, I learned what it felt like to be orphaned, even though I had been a fully functioning adult for many years. To this day, I continue to miss their presence in my life, and my thoughts often turn to all the ways in which they showed their love for me and my sister. Of all the wonderful things they did for us and taught us, I believe the greatest example of their love was exhibited through our tutelage in the ways of our Lord Jesus. As a result of this tutelage, my parents by no means turned out perfect offspring, but they did give us both the best possible tools for living our lives in faith and hope.

Neither my sister nor I have forgotten the truth we learned as small children. That very truth has helped us both to survive our parents' physical deaths. It helped us to pick up our lives and continue living them, because it gave us the assurance that all was not lost and that someday we would see our parents again. The truth our parents left with us has given us peace in the knowledge that though we are flawed human beings, imperfect in our relationships even with one another, through our relationship with Jesus we have been redeemed and forgiven.

If there is anything I regret in my relationship with my parents, with my longtime college girlfriend, and with my late beloved husband, it is that I did not always go the extra mile, nor did I always take the opportunity to tell them how much they meant to me. When I reminisce on the years spent with each of these special people, I remember mostly the good, and as such I praise the Lord for His blessings yesterday, today, and tomorrow.

I realize not everyone will approach their own imminent death—or in my case, the death of loved ones—the way I did. People handle death very differently, depending on their individual backgrounds. We grieve loss differently, and we have different defense mechanisms. While some of us turn to family and friends for support, others isolate themselves and suffer silently. Some people turn to God, while others curse Him. When I flash back on my own responses after coming face-to-face with death, I find that my *modi operandi* were sometimes ineffective as I helplessly watched both my father and mother die. I can't help but regret the times I neglected to lean harder upon the Lord, when I did not call upon Him for help, and when I foolishly relied upon my own inadequate strength. Those were the times I was at my worst, particularly as I served as caregiver to my mother in her last days.

Through this admission I hope you understand that it is okay to feel and acknowledge being overwhelmed in these situations, though it is not okay to avoid asking for help from those around you—and, more importantly, from the Lord. Critics often scoff at calling upon a God who cannot be seen, touched, or embraced. For these individuals, God is nothing more than a figment of one's imagination, a convenient crutch when life goes sour. To that I say: we are all weak in the face of death, as well as in life, and even Jesus Christ cried out to His heavenly Father as He died for us on the cross. God was there for Jesus, resurrecting Him for us. Just as God was present at Calvary, if we call on Him, He will be there for us and our loved ones.

So cry out to God, remembering that only a fool throws away his solid oak crutch before he is healed—and none of us will be fully healed until the day we return to Him. While death is the natural outcome of life, it is also a "big deal," not only for the dying but also for those loved ones involved, and certainly for our heavenly Father. While circumstances differ, as do our responses, we all share the same truth: death is a reality we cannot avoid, and the death of a loved one will irrevocably change us, either to our betterment or to our detriment.

The Story Continues

As a consequence of losing the four most significant people in my life, I believe I have made some very significant, positive changes in how I approach life and how well I love those I love. I will never be perfect at loving, but I certainly try harder to demonstrate my affections in both the simple and not-so-simple things in this life. I believe God was able to use a very difficult time in my life to teach me never to take any good thing or good person for granted.

Even after that breakthrough, God was not finished with me. After ten years of widowhood I met an amazing man, who is now my husband. That is only the beginning of the story. This amazing man, whom I had never met before, had worked many years earlier in the same professional capacity as my late husband, in the same government office in Washington DC.

In fact, very early in our marriage, my late husband mentioned my current husband's first name, stating that he was "a good man." As amazing as it was to be made privy to his opinion, it was no less amazing that I had remembered this so many years later. My current husband and I have determined there was no one else in their work division with that name—except the man I am currently married to. Indeed, my husband of three years *is* a good man— another blessing from the Lord.

Do I believe this turn of events was just a coincidence? I most certainly do not. I believe that everything that has happened in my life over the past seven decades has been orchestrated by God for my refinement—a refinement we all must go through if we are to be called His. "These trials will show if your faith is genuine. It is being tested as fire tests and purifies fine gold—though your faith is far more precious than mere gold" (1 Peter 1:7).

It was only through the power of the Holy Spirit within us both that my husband and I had the courage to enter another marriage, where total commitment to one another is absolutely necessary. We both experienced loving relationships with our deceased spouses and yet had the faith to go forward in love, even with the knowledge that one of us might once again have to endure the pain of losing the other through death. "Such love has no fear, because perfect love expels all fear" (1 John 4:18). The perfect love that Scripture speaks of is Christ's love, which we emulate through the Holy Spirit within us.

Both my husband and I profess our faith in and love for Christ every day of our lives, as we study the Word and continue our faith journey together. Since the day we said our wedding vows, God has been an integral part of our relationship. As such, we never miss a day without reminding each other how much we are loved and how blessed we feel to be a part of each other's life. For this, we both praise God.

Chapter 3

Who Has It Right?

[God] has planted eternity in the human heart.
(Ecclesiastes 3:11)

*N*ow that I've shared some of my own story, we can cast the net more broadly. In this chapter we'll present some of the more prominent belief systems from around the world that help people process life, death, and grieving.

Aspects of religion, to mention but a few, often include sacred things and places, rituals, festivals, funerary services, matrimonial services, meditation, and belief in spiritual beings and an afterlife. According to the *Encyclopedia of Religion and Ethics,* "even the oldest and the most primitive human cultures believed in the afterlife."[10] For example, the Druids of the British Isles and the Egyptians of the Middle East both left behind a storehouse of religious clues (including Stonehenge and the Great Pyramids, respectively), suggesting their belief in and preparation for an afterlife.

About ten thousand religions are practiced worldwide today, with nearly 84 percent of the world's population affiliated with one of the five most commonly practiced religions.[11] Nearly all religions profess a belief in a god(s) and an afterlife. For the purpose of this book, we will examine only the faiths most commonly ascribed to—Buddhism, Hinduism, New Age, Judaism, Christianity, and Islam—and focus on each religion's view on death, the afterlife, and immortality.

Buddhism

The ultimate spiritual goal for the Buddhist is to achieve *nirvana* (enlightenment). To accomplish this, the faithful are required to live many lives and experience many deaths. Enlightenment for the Buddhist is that state in which one relinquishes a focus upon self to attain a state of *no-self*. Buddhists believe that only within the *no-self* state will one achieve release from sadness and striving. Numerous sources can serve to guide the faithful to reach enlightenment. Instructive guides will almost always focus upon *right understanding, right thought, right speech, right action, right livelihood, right effort, right mindfulness,* and *right concentration.*[12]

Within the Buddhist philosophy the predominant objective is to achieve an enlightened state in which the painful aspects of this life—including aging, illness, and death—are of little concern. The existence of a creator God and a human soul is not considered, and neither is recognized within the Buddhist faith. Even the faith's founder, Siddhartha Gautama (or Buddha Gautama, or simply the Buddha), is not revered as a god but is looked upon as a mortal being who reached the state of enlightenment.

As for what transpires at the point of death for those who have not yet reached enlightenment, there are various versions of Buddhist belief. One version of what might occur following death can be found within *The Tibetan Book of the Dead*, which details various stages of the afterlife experience that eventually lead to either reincarnation or enlightenment.[13] As the Buddhist faith does not support belief in an eternal soul, one version of reincarnation teaching holds that positive karma (good deeds) enters the newborn physical body, while another version supports the belief that the deceased's consciousness (sensations, emotions, and perceptions) is what enters the newborn physical body.

In any event, some aspect of the former person is believed to continue on after death, at least until reaching the point of enlightenment or nirvana. Once nirvana is achieved, it is unclear what final destination the remaining remnant of past lives might take, whether complete extinction or unification with a central energy force.

Hinduism

Buddhism shares many beliefs and practices with Hinduism. This is not at all surprising, as Gautama Buddha, the

Buddhist founder, had been born and raised a Hindu.[14]
Those shared beliefs include a belief in karma and reincarnation, entailing the need to die with good karma in order
to escape returning to the world stage of sadness and suffering. This is known as the *Saṃsāra cycle*.

Despite the similarities, there are differences as well.
For instance, Hindus believe in the existence of an eternal human soul, known as the *atman*. Hinduism also supports a belief in the God-creator, or *Brahma*. Lesser gods
are worshiped as well, as the faith allows for as many as
330,000,000 other gods.[15] Though a soul will undergo a
cycle of many deaths and rebirths, the ultimate goal, as
within the Aviate Vedanta tradition, is for a soul to achieve
nirvana, which represents a state of complete oneness with
Brahma.[16] At this point, the Saṃsāra cycle comes to an end.

New Age Spirituality

Western new age spirituality is a direct descendant of the
Buddhist and Hindu traditions. The philosophy ascribes to
a belief in reincarnation and human divinity and is both
pantheistic and monistic in practice.[17] Through misinterpreted Christian Scripture, as well as through advances
within quantum physics, the New Age movement continues to claim support for its worldview.[18] (I will discuss new
insights revealed through quantum physics in Chapter 6.)

New age spirituality makes no distinction between the
Creator and the creation. God is seen as being in everything and everyone, and therefore everything and everyone

is god, including every man, woman, and child. New Agers believe in life after death, and that the final destination will be reached only after many reincarnations. Specifically, the final destination is achieving oneness with the universal mind, rather than an individual consciousness spent with a personal God. Because there is no distinction between good or evil, all share the same fate.

Judaism

Judaism was established 3,500 years ago and is the oldest of the three major monotheistic religions (Judaism, Christianity, and Islam). The Jewish Torah teaches without question the existence of the one and only omnipotent, personal God. Throughout Judaism's long history, various factions within the faith have been at odds concerning the validity of life beyond the grave, as well as what that life might entail. While the Sadducees rejected all concepts concerning survival beyond the grave, the Pharisees believed that virtuous souls continued to a nondescript, blessed destiny. Within the Pharisees' framework, those proven unworthy were thought to go on to ceaseless torment.[19]

Historically, Judaism has failed to recognize Jesus Christ as its long-awaited Messiah, consequently the same debate continues within the faith today. The four main branches of Judaism differ in their belief in life beyond the grave, the resurrection of the body, and other specifics as to what might take place at the end of life. The four major branches of the faith are Orthodox, Reform, Conservative, and Reconstructionist. While Orthodox Judaism affirms belief in life after death as well as a bodily messianic resurrection, the Reform branch believes in the divine nature of the human spirit, though it rejects a belief in heaven and hell as well as the concept of a bodily resurrection. Conservative Judaism serves as a compromise between the Orthodox and Reform branches of the faith, professing a belief in the continuing existence of the individual soul after death. Meanwhile, as a segment of the Reform movement, Reconstructionism lends itself to the belief that neither resurrection nor immortality is "integral to the Jewish religion," while others within this group assert that upon death a soul returns to the universe.[20]

That said, within the four branches of Judaism themselves it is common to find differing opinions on the afterlife amongst both followers and religious leaders. The question of life after death remains more a central focus within the two remaining monotheistic religions, Christianity and Islam, both of which find their roots within Judaism.

Christianity

The two-thousand-year-old monotheistic faith of Christianity includes three main branches: Roman Catholicism, Protestantism, and Greek Orthodox. The foundation of Christianity rests upon the crucifixion and resurrection of Jesus Christ, as prophesied throughout Jewish Scripture. Though considered true to the monotheistic God of the Jews, the Christian God is seen as triune in nature—encompassing the Father, the Son, and the Holy Spirit, referred to as the Trinity. Orthodox Christians of all denominations believe that Jesus Christ is divine and that He represents the Son of God within the Trinity.

The Christian Old Testament Bible is derived directly from the *Tanakh*, the Hebrew Bible. Throughout Jewish Scripture, there are references to the coming and suffering of a Messiah. One such reference is found in Exodus 12:1–51, which prophesies that the Messiah would be the Passover Lamb. The many messianic prophecies foretelling the coming of a Jewish Messiah and liberator are too numerous to include in this brief synopsis; the Human Truth Foundation provides a detailed listing within both the Hebrew Scriptures and the Christian Bible across different traditions.[21]

The historic record shows that while some Jews of ancient times recognized Jesus Christ as their Messiah, others did not. Henceforth, a small band of Jews and Gentiles who came to believe that Jesus Christ was the long-awaited Messiah would become the first known Christians. The very foundation of this newfound faith is the belief that one's salvation can only be achieved through a professed belief in the death and resurrection of Jesus Christ. Only through the Christ of the Bible will the human soul be washed clean of sin and made acceptable to be received by God into his heavenly realm upon death. Because the human soul is believed to be eternal, those not cleansed of their sin through the acceptance of Jesus Christ as their personal Savior are doomed to spend eternity separated from God and subject to the forces of evil.

Islam

Of the three monotheistic religions, Islam is the most recent, having been established through the prophet Mohammed between 570 and 632 AD.[22] There are many similarities and many differences among Islam, Judaism, and Christianity. While the Islamic faith believes in one God, Allah, they do not recognize the Christian Trinity. Islam holds that neither the Islamic prophet Mohammed nor Jesus Christ are divine—a distinction that rests with Allah (God) alone. Followers of Islam do believe in life after death, as well as an eternal soul who eventually enters either heaven or hell.

The Quran, the Islamic book of religious authority, states that every soul shall taste of death.[23] Like the Jews and the Christians, followers of Islam believe that God alone gives life and takes it away. The faiths soon part ways, however, in that Islam (not unlike Judaism) teaches that entrance into paradise (heaven) is achieved through good works and living a worthy life rather than through God's grace. All three faiths believe that the human soul is eternal and that those not accepted into heaven will descend into hell. Islam also teaches that there are various levels of both heaven and hell, which are far more involved than those described in Roman Catholic theology.

A Common Thread

In examining each of these religions, one interesting aspect is not necessarily the tenets of one religion versus another—but rather, that there appears to be an innate need within humans to seek out something or someone to worship for the sake of making sense out of this life. The relentless universal drive to answer the unanswerable appears to be hardwired into our DNA.

When we examine the most commonly practiced religions, we find that all but Buddhists believe in at least one deity and/or creator. In addition, all religions promote the belief that some aspect of the former self survives beyond the grave. Moreover, the Austin Institute of Family and Culture conducted a 2014 study of 15,738 Americans who considered themselves either agnostics or atheists, regarding their belief in an afterlife. Somewhat surprisingly, of those who participated, 32 percent identified themselves as having a belief in some form of an afterlife. From the same study, 6 percent of agnostics and atheists stated that *they believed in a bodily resurrection.*[24]

Where Do We Go from Here?

So, do all paths lead to heaven? With great fortitude, humankind has pondered this question throughout history. While most hold fast to the exclusiveness of their own brand of worship and doctrine in bringing them closer to the divine and heaven, only universalists believe that all paths lead to heaven and that eventually all of mankind will be saved. In the end, faith is based upon more than the visible—and the invisible makes test-tube empirical evidence hard to come by.

On a superficial level, the reasons for subscribing to any one of the ten thousand religions of the world seem relatively obvious.[25] Most of us practice the religion we were raised in, or at least we give that religion lip service—though there are rare occasions in history and within individual lives when thought precipitates action and true faith takes hold of us. Not to be discouraged, humankind continues to work toward finding the truth we all crave.

Bear in mind that within contemporary education truth is recognized as being relative, meaning that it is considered personal and not objective. Even so, Christianity was founded upon one objective truth—God's truth—and as such remains and always will be incompatible with any other worldview. That being the case, it would be a contradiction to state that other worldviews are true as well. When the evidence we require is slow in coming, we often look toward our theologians of today and yesterday for affirmation that we are on the right track. As Timothy Keller states in his bestselling book *The Reason for God*, regardless whether one subscribes to atheism, universalism, Judaism, Hinduism, Christianity, or any other "worldview," the decision is based upon faith alone.[26] Unless we are able to identify a common thread, this conclusion might seem to lead us nowhere.

Again, the common thread that runs through the world religions (with the exception of Buddhism) is a belief in a God as well as a belief in the continuation of life beyond the grave. Humans share within their DNA a longsuffering for empirical proof that they have a heavenly Father and that the life given them is eternal. No one offers greater insight into this amazing relationship we all have with the Creator of the universe than C. S. Lewis:

> A wish may lead to false beliefs, granted. But what does the existence of the wish suggest? At one time I was much impressed by Arnold's line "Nor does the being hungry prove that we have bread." But surely, [though] it doesn't prove that one particular man will get food, it does prove that there is such a thing as food! . . . [I]f we were a species that didn't normally eat, weren't designed to eat, [would] we feel hungry?[27]

It is doubtful that humankind would have gone to the lengths it has throughout history to seek out God and heaven if they did not exist. I believe we all seek God and heaven from the moment of birth. The truth that there is a God and heaven is the only thing that will fill the hole within each and every one of us. God is the truth who transcends all proof, and He alone will sustain us through the best and worst of times this side of eternity, even unto death. Never stop looking for God—for when you find Him, you will understand the reason for your own dogged search.

Chapter 4

The Process of Dying

And the last enemy to be destroyed is death.
(1 Corinthians 15:26)

*T*hanatology, the study of death, is nothing new to the world of science. Throughout history, scientists have strived to understand whether death is programmed within living structures, where death came from, and why living organisms and their cells are not immortal. Natural death, versus death due to accidents and other means of inflicted violence, is distinguishable in terms of immortality. In their book *The Biology of Death*, Andre Klarsfeld and Frederic Revah explain the enigmatic nature of death:

> The existence of aging and natural death does not result from any particular advantage that it may have for an individual or for a species. We suggest that natural death has no value in and of itself;

its existence is simply the result of a central biological pointlessness to repair systems that would
prevent aging. All organisms are doomed to exist
temporarily, because they are perishable.[28]

That said, if natural death is indeed pointless, that
would seem to lend credence to the biblical truth that God
never meant for man to die a physical death, but rather that
death arrived on the scene along with original sin.

The Two Stages of Death

Contrary to what Hollywood movies might have us
believe, a person's transition from life to death is not typi-
cally instantaneous but rather a process that can take hours
to complete.[29] A side effect of being born into this world
is cellular death, a process that takes place over a period of
time. Numerous events might trigger the process of cellular
death, most often an illness or accident. Many physiological changes occur between the state of life and death, with
not only medical ramifications but legal, ethical, philo-
sophical, and spiritual as well.

The process of dying occurs in two stages: *clinical death,*
and then, *biological death.* During the progression toward
biological death, brain and cellular death begin at different
rates.[30]

Stage 1—Clinical death occurs when an individual's heart stops beating and breathing has ceased.

Consequently, oxygen and nutrients are no longer being circulated throughout the body. This is
a crucial stage because if the heart is not restarted
and/or breathing does not resume via CPR (car-
diopulmonary resuscitation) or other necessary
first aid within four to six minutes, brain cells will
begin to die.[31]

Stage 2—Biological death ensues when medical/
first aid interventions are either not sufficient or
not applied in a timely fashion. Within fifteen to
twenty minutes, brain cell loss becomes extensive
due to oxygen deprivation.[32] Soon after, other
cells within the body begin to die. Beyond six
to eight hours blood cells within the body start
to lose their oxygen-carrying capabilities, prior
to that time frame the blood remains sterile and
able to carry oxygen.[33] In certain instances such
as cold-water drownings, body cells will remain
viable longer than normal. Therefore, it becomes
prudent to continue life-support efforts well
beyond any predefined time limit.

No matter what caused the heart and breathing to
stop (whether acute trauma or cardiovascular disease), it
is imperative that a normal heartbeat and respiration be
restored quickly to sustain life. Through implementing
CPR, cooling down the body, and blocking the chemical
catalysts within the brain and other organs that precipitate
cellular death, medical science has reached the point where

the dying process can be slowed down or even halted. Under these conditions, it is estimated that bone cells are viable up to four days, skin cells for twenty-four hours, and fat cells up to thirteen hours; in addition, nerve cells and brain tissue remain reversible for up to eight hours.[34]

Power over Death

One would be hard-pressed not to applaud the dedicated men and women of science who have strived against great odds to prolong human life. Statistics from the American Heart Association indicate that heart disease remains the number-one cause of death within the United States. Some 790,000 people will suffer heart-related illnesses every year, leading to 114,000 deaths. Despite this gloomy projection, the annual coronary heart disease death rate declined 35.5 percent between 2004 and 2014, no doubt attributable to first responders and advanced medical technology.[35] Certainly, in the interest of all mankind, men and women of science will continue in their noble quest to eradicate death stemming not only from heart disease but all other causes as well.

Advancements made through medical science, including worldwide availability of sophisticated technology, has steadily lured humankind into the false hope that science rather than God will eventually eradicate death. While prolonging life can be a blessing, it may also come with many ethical and spiritual challenges not only for physicians but the patient and family as well. We would do well to take note of the predicament portrayed in the noted play *Death Takes a Holiday.* Prince Sirki, alias the "Shadow of Death," reminds humankind "I am the gateway to life that leads beyond life."[36] Chillingly, it is hard to imagine what might occur should man rather than God destroy death, while at the same time having no ability to eradicate sin as well. The Bible saints witnessed for us that all will happen in God's time, and that in this life or in eternity, separation from God is far worse than physical death. That being the case, might extended life under these conditions be little more than a living hell?

On the other hand, many who have experienced a Near Death Experience (NDE) witnessed for a place they did not necessarily want to leave—not even to return to life and loved ones. In the next chapter I share some of those documented encounters with God and the afterlife.

Chapter 5

From Death and Back

Letting your sinful nature control your mind leads to death. But letting the spirit control your mind leads to life and peace. (Romans 8:6)

Reports of near-death experiences (NDEs) have existed throughout history. For instance, the classical Greek philosopher Plato wrote the *Republic*, an account of a soldier named Er who returns from death with a story of leaving his body and traveling to a place where he is judged.[37] Other historical notables who have reported their own near-death experiences include Carl Jung, Thomas Edison, and Ernest Hemingway.[38]

As discussed, through advances in medical science and technology it is possible to sustain the clinically dead for weeks, months, and even years in a state of limbo, neither fully alive nor dead. This has had an unexpected result: medical professionals are now first in line for reports from

beyond the grave. As a consequence, even hardcore natural-
ists in the field of medicine and natural science have had to
take note that something without explanation, well beyond
the limits of Newtonian physics, continues to take place.

Studies of Near-Death Experience (NDE)

As early as the nineteenth century, the rigors of scientific
study have been applied to the phenomenon of the near-
death experience (NDE).[39] From 1975 to the present, many
physicians and scientists have been involved with either
retrospective or prospective studies pertaining to NDEs.
Retrospective studies focus on individuals who experienced
an NDE in the past and then share their recollections with
researchers. Prospective studies often include hospital-
ized resuscitated patients, who provide the researcher with
NDE information both before and after it occurs. Given
the many advantages of the prospective approach, more
studies are being conducted using this model.[40]

Many of these studies have been generated through the
International Association for Near Death Studies (IANDS),
an organization based in Durham, North Carolina (www.
iands.org). Additional research centers include the Loui-
siana-based Near Death Experience Research Foundation
and those at the University of Connecticut, the University
of North Texas, and the Division of Perceptual Studies at
the University of Virginia. In the United Kingdom, South-
ampton University has been a forerunner in researching
NDEs.[41]

Many distinguished physicians and scientists have also dedicated years to researching NDEs. Pioneers in this field include Elizabeth Kubler-Ross, Raymond Moody, P. M. H. Atwater, Bruce Greyson, Melvin Morse, Peter Fenwick, Sam Parnia, Michael Sabom, Jeffrey Long, Pim van Lommel, and Kenneth Ring.[42] The research of these pioneers, and the firsthand accounts of those who claim to have had a glimpse of the afterlife and returned to tell about it, has generated numerous books, as well as both scholarly and popular articles.

Of the many books written on the subject, most include the criteria by which researchers authenticate an individual's report of having had an NDE. An NDE may include all or some of the following elements listed in Jeffrey Long's book *Evidence of the Afterlife*:

1. Out-of-body experience (OBE): Separation of consciousness from the physical body

2. Heightened senses

3. Intense and generally positive emotions or feelings

4. Passing into or through a tunnel

5. Encountering a mystical or brilliant light

6. Encountering other beings, either mystical beings or deceased relatives or friends

7. A sense of alteration of time or space

8. Life review

9. Encountering unworldly ("heavenly") realms

10. Encountering or learning special knowledge

11. Encountering a boundary or barrier
12. A return to the body, either voluntary or involuntary[43]

A Widespread Experience

It would be difficult to calculate, or even imagine, what percentage of the US or world population might have experienced an NDE within a specific span of time. Yet through compilation of data gathered in several major surveys involving US adults, a Gallup Poll estimated that in 1992 alone, 13 million Americans had experienced an NDE. At that time the adult population of the US was approximately 260 million, meaning that 5 percent of the population had experienced an NDE that year.[44]

Research evidence shows that people change after experiencing an NDE, and most of the changes observed were beneficial to both the individual and society. The vast majority of those who had experienced an NDE appeared to be more self-confident, had a stronger sense of spirituality, were far less interested in material gain and status, and placed a greater value upon the needs of others and the sacredness of life.[45] Post-NDErs also appeared to have a stronger sense of God in their lives as well as a reduced fear of death than they felt prior to the NDE.[46]

P. M. H. Atwater, an NDE researcher who herself survived an NDE, places a somewhat different spin on the return to earthly reality from paradise. She states that upon returning from an NDE, there is always a period of transition when one is forced to rediscover one's self and reclaim his or her earthly life. Dr. Atwater states that this endeavor, which can last anywhere from hours to even years, can be stressful.[47]

According to studies generated by IANDS, not every NDE is filled with light and love, and 1–15 percent of NDEs in 2001 were described as distressing.[48] Jeffrey Long, author of *God and the Afterlife,* describes distressing NDEs as having one or more of the following characteristics: *frightening, a sense of nonexistence or a frightening void, and graphic hellish imagery.*[49] The life transformation that takes place following a distressing NDE can be even more dramatic than that which often occurs following a positive NDE.

One of the more life-changing NDEs occurred when artist and teacher Howard Storm died and was transported into what could only be construed as the bowels of hell. He described his terrifying experience in great detail in his book *My Descent into Death.*[50] A confirmed atheist, Storm reports that as he struggled with the demons of hell, he recalled his childhood prayers and called out to Jesus for rescue. Almost immediately he was encompassed by an entity of light that he identified as Jesus. Despite the medical emergency, which should have killed him hours earlier, he was restored to life.

What followed the NDE was every bit as amazing as the NDE itself. Once a man focused upon self-centered achievement and materialism, Storm was transformed into a person focused on meeting the needs of others and in quest of his own spiritual fulfillment. Like many others who have experienced an NDE, Howard Storm changed his profession. After spending twenty years of his life as a studio art professor in a university setting, he eventually attended seminary and currently serves as pastor of a church in Ohio.

People of all faiths throughout the world have reported experiencing NDEs. The vast majority of NDErs provide descriptions of what heaven is like, that are relatively consistent. The features of heaven most NDErs report are supported by the tenets of the world's major religions. These features include an out-of-body experience, the tunnel experience, life reviews, the *realm of light,* a being of light, and the presence of the deceased.[51] For details pertaining to the religious texts that support the version of heaven as described by NDErs, refer to the *Handbook of Near-Death Experiences: Thirty Years of Investigation,* edited by Janice Miner Holden, Debbie James, and Bruce Greyson.

Are NDEs Biblical?

The Christian faith remains guarded in its willingness to recognize the NDE experience as an experience generated through the triune God. The main objection is that many of the reported NDEs appear incompatible with the stated beliefs of Christianity, based in the scriptural authority of the Holy Bible. That authority calls for a belief in the triune God, in Jesus Christ as God incarnate, and in Jesus' redemptive death and resurrection to cleanse humanity of its sin. The Bible plainly states that Jesus alone is the pathway to God and eternity: "I am the way, the truth, and the life. No one can come to the Father except through me" (John 14:6). Concerns arise when NDErs fail to identify the being of light as Jesus Christ and instead identify the light in terms of their own religion.

At a cursory glance NDEs might appear to favor the universalist understanding that all roads lead to God and heaven rather than a single road, namely the redemptive nature of Jesus Christ alone. Consequently, many Christians interpret such a message as demonic in nature, citing Scripture as a reminder that "Satan disguises himself as an angel of light" (2 Corinthians 11:14). For the moment, the *modus operandi* for the Christian community is to judge each NDE on its own merits and condemn any doctrine that denies biblical authority while deeming those that give testimony to Jesus Christ and his exclusive redemptive powers as touched by the hand of God.[52]

The Verdict

Authors and scientists alike are cautioned to remain unbiased while pursuing a truth either through the pen or the test tube. Given the nature of this book, I believe I would be remiss not to include my personal beliefs and how I have come to terms with relatively recent revelations. I have no doubt whatsoever that God incarnate through the personage of Jesus Christ visited earth some two thousand years ago and at that time accomplished all that was set before Him. In so doing, Jesus revealed Himself as being far more than the seed of Christianity but as the Creator of all and the gateway to an eternity with God.

Though Christians are cautioned not to transfer their hope for eternity from the truth of the Bible to the second-hand reports of NDErs, many NDEs do more to support the tenets of the faith than not.[53] I believe in the infallibility of the Holy Bible, including prophecy which continues to be fulfilled to the present day. Nevertheless, God's Word as written in the Holy Bible is but a primer for those of us living on this earth, and only in God's eternity will all His truths be revealed to us. Through the Bible we learn that Jesus Christ is unconditional love. As His followers, we are commissioned to emulate that same love here on earth. I believe there are people from all walks of life, as well as all religions, who know Jesus' love and practice it.[54] Upon death, all will be judged with the same consistency and mercy that Jesus practiced when He walked this earth. On all else, I reserve comment.

While not all the messages from heaven as reported by NDErs conform to what one might have learned or imagined, overall they have resulted in the dispersion of more good than evil throughout the world. For instance, Maurice Rawlings (1978) reported through his research that atheists and agnostics who experienced an NDE became convinced that there was more to life than their material existence, and that not only did God exist but that there was life beyond the grave.[55] With the realization that an individual's search for truth and meaning in this world is on a continuum, belief in God is certainly a step in the right direction.

Far less dramatic, though certainly more common, are the NDErs' heightened appreciation for their past religious practices and all things of a spiritual nature. For instance, although Dr. Eben Alexander attended church, only after his NDE did he experience those sensations of awe and wonder in worshiping his Creator. The impact of Dr. Alexander's NDE was experienced not only by himself, but his story also touched the lives of those physicians within his medical community.

Miraculously, Dr. Alexander recovered fully from an antibiotic-resistant strain of bacterial meningitis. Alexander, a neurosurgeon, is certainly one of the bluebloods of academia. He earned his medical degrees at Duke University Medical School, Newcastle-Upon-Tyne in the United Kingdom, and Harvard University and was not easily swayed into believing even his own emotions. While experiencing his NDE, Alexander had a fascinating encounter with a sister he never knew on this side of the veil, which he was forced to come to terms with upon his return.

As he explains in his book *Proof of Heaven,* in order to satisfy his own skepticism concerning what he had experienced, Alexander went about scientifically ruling out any possible physiological reason for his NDE. With the understanding that the neocortex of his brain was not functional during his illness and that this area of the brain is vital to sensory perception, generation of motor commands, spatial reasoning, conscious thought, and language, Alexander methodically began to rule out possible physiological reasons for his experience.

The neuroscientific hypotheses Alexander had ruled out included: 1) a primitive brainstem program in response to terminal pain and suffering, 2) a drug-induced psychedelic event, 3) a distorted recall of memories from the limbic system, 4) REM intrusion, 5) "DMT dump," and 6) "reboot phenomenon."[56] For any of the first five hypotheses to be the cause of Dr. Alexander's NDE, the neocortex of his brain would have had to be functioning, and it was not. The sixth possible explanation was ruled most unlikely to be the cause of such intricate recollections as the kind Alexander experienced.[57]

To date, no one has uncovered a physiologic explanation for NDEs that satisfies the rigors of the scientific method. NDEs join a long list of spiritual phenomena that includes miracles, not excluding Christ's resurrection, which has remained unexplainable in light of man's archaic science. Is it at all possible that God continues to have a hand in it all?

One final NDE particularly relevant to the following chapter was documented in Dr. Jeffrey Long's book *God and the Afterlife.* While visiting an Oregon beach, a fourteen-year-old girl named Demi stepped into a sinkhole that trapped her within the sand. At first she fought desperately to free herself but soon lapsed into a state of total peace and love. During her NDE she was told that the most important thing in the universe is love, and that she was like everything else within the universe, including though not limited to a blade of grass.

Years later she attended college, and though she studied both the biological sciences and physics, she continued to remain stymied concerning her NDE revelation. Then she stumbled upon a TV program on quantum physics that explained how everything in the universe, whether animate or inanimate, is composed of the same energy. At that point Demi finally understood the meaning behind the perplexing message about her likeness with everything else in the universe.[58]

Just as Demi was able to pull the pieces of her NDE together as a consequence of her fleeting encounter with a basic concept of quantum physics, and just as it has held significance in my own search, I hope it will for you as well. I'm sure Demi would agree that it is a blessing to live during the twenty-first century, a time when God has chosen to leave His handprint in some of the most unexpected places. As prophesied within the Holy Bible, we have entered a time of rapid technological change that has opened the opportunity for further enlightenment as to God's omnipotent and omniscient presence within every aspect of this world and beyond. The best is yet to come!

Chapter 6

The Omniscient God

So we fix our eyes not on what is seen, but on what is unseen, since what is seen is temporary, but what is unseen is eternal. (2 Corinthians 4:18, NIV)

*H*ave you ever entertained the thought that what we interpret as miraculous is actually God's science at work? The very miracles we stand in awe of at some point may very well be empirically explained through science. Rather than diminishing our astonishment, our newfound understanding might very well place the focus of our awe more so upon the Giver than upon the gift!

For many years, the paradigm that science is somehow adversarial to spirituality has been widely accepted. This notion has been fostered largely through Newtonian physics. The main focus of Newtonian physics rests upon the visible universe and how forces therein act upon matter.[59] Any force that is measurable, such as energy, is considered to be visible. Intertwined with Newtonian physics were two widely accepted viewpoints, material-ism and naturalism, which are often confused as being identical. Materialism is the viewpoint that nothing exists outside of matter, while naturalism holds that everything can be explained in terms of "natural causes and laws."[60] As stated, though energy is not visible to the naked eye, it is measurable, thereby falling within the Newtonian first law of thermodynamics. The law of thermodynamics states that energy can neither be created nor destroyed, but only transformed. The very nature of energy may well have been a precursor to discoveries yet to come.[61] By the 1900s quantum physics began to come into its own, mov-ing science slowly from the visible to the invisible, from the temporary to the eternal. Today quantum physics, also referred to as quantum mechanics, has shaken the materialistic/naturalistic position to its very core.

An Introduction to Quantum Physics

While most of us may not understand the mathemati-cal equations of quantum physics, it is possible to reach a modicum of understanding of its basic concepts. Quan-tum physics is the study of subatomic particles. All mat-ter—whether in the form of people, plants, animals, rocks, stars, or planets—is made up of cells, which in turn con-tain molecules made from microscopic atoms.[62] An atom is composed of a nucleus, neutrons, protons, and electrons. In order to travel into the world of quantum physics, scientists must go even smaller into the workings of those composite particles within the atom. And so they have, discovering that the electron is composed of "leptons," while the protons and neutrons are made up of "quarks."[63] Quarks were once believed to be the smallest components of a cell known to man, until the string theorists challenged that model. The string theorists go even smaller, claiming that quarks and leptons are made up of vibrating energy referred to as *strings*.[64]

So what is the significance of quantum elements within the atom—and what, if anything, do they have to do with God and heaven? These elements are the smallest of the small, representing packets of energy. Every living and non-living thing within the universe is composed of these invisible packets of energy. If you recall, according to the laws of thermodynamics, energy can never be destroyed. Therefore, science has afforded us the confidence that at the very least, a small invisible part of us is undoubtedly eternal.

Quantum characteristics point to a multidimensional, subatomic world far more complex and mercurial than that of the macroscopic world we know. For instance, the zaniness of the atomic and subatomic world is displayed through the discovery of *wave-particle duality*.[65] Repeated experiments have shown that a single electron has the capacity to transform itself from energy to solid matter depending solely upon whether or not it is observed. When observed, an invisible energy wave converts into a visible particle, while unobserved it reverts to the invisible energy wave. If indeed this is how matter might have come into existence, the logical question that follows is: Who, or what, served as the initial observer?

The Christian Bible tells us that the sovereign God created both the invisible and the visible (Colossians 1:16); for the Christian it would be no stretch of the imagination to believe that the divine God of the Bible had been and continues to be that Observer.

The very fact that the quantum world is *non-local* in nature also smacks of the hand of God. This means that unlike the *local* world we currently occupy, the quantum world cannot be localized in time and space.[66] How do we know that? Following extensive experimentation, physicists have uncovered general properties of all *quanta* (energy), which confirm its *nonlocality*. A few of those noted properties include *quantum entanglement, tunneling, and teleportation.*

Quantum entanglement occurs when a proton passes through matter, causing the proton to decay into two new protons, together having the same energy equivalent as that of the original proton. These two new protons are *entangled* for life. What happens to one proton instantaneously happens to the other, regardless whether they are in close proximity or galaxies apart. Their communication occurs faster than the speed of light. The entanglement phenomenon literally flies in the face of time and space. Entanglement is a literal demonstration of the capability of being in two places at one time and involves two or more particles with the same capability working as one system.[67]

Quantum tunneling is another characteristic within the quantum physics world that illustrates nonlocality. Very simply this is the ability of an atomic particle to dematerialize and then rematerialize on the opposite side of a barrier at speeds faster than the speed of light.[68] Quantum teleportation involves the ability of an object to dematerialize in one location, only to transfer its configuration to another location, where it then reconstructs itself.[69]

Quantum physics illustrates how this phenomenon occurs routinely within the invisible quantum world, and if transposed into our visible world, certainly would qualify as "miraculous." Secular author Brian Clegg took note of this *implication* and referred to quantum entanglement as the God Effect.[70] Whether or not Clegg actually sees a personal God behind the scenes is debatable.

For those who have experienced a miracle or who know someone who has, the belief that God might have had something to do with the event usually does not appear farfetched. In her book *Heaven's Reality Lifting the Quantum Veil,* theoretical quantum physicist Dr. Sarah McGee states that there is no reason not to believe that "God can easily change the configuration of the quantum waves to change the visible state of things we can see, to do miracles without violating any of the laws of nature."[71] This is a plausible truth that people of faith have always believed—and one that those of the secular world are now forced to struggle with.

Chapter 7

Miracles, Great and Small

"Unless you people see signs and wonders," Jesus told him, "you will never believe." (John 4:48)

Many books have been written about miracles, taking varying approaches in defining and explaining what miracles are and what impact they have upon humankind. Webster's dictionary defines a miracle as "an extraordinary event manifesting divine intervention in human affairs."[72] C. S. Lewis lent his own understanding of a miracle as "something unique that breaks a pattern so expected and established we hardly consider the possibility that it could be broken."[73]

Miracles and World Religions

Miracles have their place within all five of the world's major religions as well as among New Age adherents. Rather than approaching the miraculous from the standpoint of an all-powerful magnanimous God meeting the immediate needs of His creation, some authors have chosen to present miracles in the context of the belief system of the religion the miracle is associated with. For instance, those miracles presented in the Hebrew Bible are seen as primarily occurring from the perspective of establishing the Israelites as God's chosen and covenanted people.[74] Within Christianity, Jesus' miracles are seen as a way in which to usher the reappearance of God into the world. Through performing miracles that only God could do, Jesus cemented both His divine and human nature for His observers. While the miracles of the New Testament are performed by Jesus and later his apostles, only Christ's resurrection is identified as a miracle without intercession and solely of God the Father. The resurrection miracle serves as the very foundation of the Christian faith, while also reinforcing the conceptual belief in the Father, Son, and Holy Spirit, as the Christian triune God.[75]

While there remain sects within the Islamic faith that do not subscribe to the faith's reported miracles, others do recognize the miracles believed to have been performed through Muhammad. Muhammad, commonly referred to as the Prophet, attributed his miracles to the power of God or Allah. For the most part Muhammad's miracles helped to emphasize the meaning of pivotal events in his life as well as the importance of specific doctrine.[76] The faithful consider the Quran to be its faith's greatest miracle, and while Muhammad is revered, the reverence has less to do with his miracles than with what his followers see as his exemplary life.[77]

Though neither Hinduism nor Buddhism subscribe to a personal God, there exist factions within both faiths that do recognize miracles. Buddha was reported to have performed miracles, though miracles as such were not at the core of his ministry. Within these two Eastern faiths there exists considerable overlap as to how miracles are interpreted. For instance, both faiths see miracles as signs of transcendent wisdom, as well as of the impermanence of the material world.[78] In keeping with the concept of liberation of self as the final goal within both these faiths, humans who transcend the idea of self are believed to be free from the constraints of the laws of nature, to the point of being able to perform their own miracles.[79] In line with this concept, those who ascribe to new age spirituality believe that miracles can be realized through the proper use of one's divine mind.[80]

Worldwide, people of all faiths have reported either experiencing miracles themselves or believing in their occurrence. In his book *The Book of Miracles*, Kenneth L. Woodward reports that within the US, "Opinion polls continue to show that 82 percent of the population believes that God continues to work miracles."[81] This is not as surprising as it might seem. Despite the impact of secularism throughout American culture, eight out of ten Americans continue to identify with the Christian worldview. Of all the world religions, Christianity more often incorporates miracles of God throughout both the Old and New Testaments of its Holy Bible.[82]

Those touched by a miracle are often left awestricken, as though caught up in a shower of star dust. Others wait, vicariously believing yet not quite ready to acknowledge the miracles within their own lives. Lastly, are those who are intent upon not being duped despite all the evidence, aligning themselves with the wit of Mark Twain in believing that faith itself is nothing more than "believing what you know just ain't so." These are the same folks who look to science to explain how the inconceivable might have occurred. Certainly, all of these reactions come with their own justification.

Biblical Miracles and Quantum Physics

Again, those recent discoveries in the field of quantum physics show promise in bridging the gap between believer and cynic. Theoretical quantum physicist Dr. Sarah A. McGee lends credence to the establishment of such a bridge: "God has made the laws of nature so flexible that He can do any miracle He wants without violating any of the rules."[83]

One of the more fascinating attributes of the quantum world is its duality, being both a wave (the nonmaterial state) and a particle (the material state), interchangeably. When observed through experimentation, the dematerialized wave collapses into a materialized particle.[84] The implications are mind-boggling when one ponders the fact that all matter, including *Homo sapiens*, are made up of the same quantum elements, possessing the attribute of wave/particle duality.

This characteristic, as well as other aspects of quantum physics, were made manifest through the miracles of Jesus Christ. For instance, quantum duality is evident when Jesus mysteriously dematerializes in order to escape an angry crowd (John 8:59). On two other occasions Jesus escaped being stoned (John 10:31, 39) and later being thrown from a cliff (Luke 4:28–30) through the same means.[85] Another miracle Jesus performed after His resurrection exemplifies His ability to change quantum realities so that His personage was able to tunnel through a locked door so he might fellowship with His disciples (John 20:25–29).[86] Jesus demonstrated nonlocality, another characteristic of quantum physics, through the healing of the centurion soldier's servant. At the request of a Roman centurion, Jesus heals his servant at a distance far removed from where the two men spoke. The centurion implored Jesus: "Just say the word from where you are, and my servant will be healed" (Luke 7:7). Due to the centurion's faith, Jesus healed his servant.[87]

Throughout His three years of earthly ministry, Jesus performed many healings, exorcisms, the feeding of thousands, materializing and dematerializing, walking on water, as well as resurrecting the dead. With all of these miracles, Jesus always acknowledged His Father in heaven: "I tell you the truth; the Son can do nothing by himself. He does only what he sees the Father doing. Whatever the Father does, the Son also does" (John 5:19). Jesus' resurrection and ascension were miracles performed directly through the hand of God—and changed the world! This incredible miracle surely shows God's ultimate power, a power to levitate and lift from the grave His dead Son, returning Him to life and to the invisible realm of heaven.[88] Taking God at His Word, can we expect anything less for ourselves if we but believe on the Son?

Just as Jesus shared in God's omnipotent power in order to perform miracles, later Jesus' apostles through the Holy Spirit were given the ability to perform miracles. Today, across the globe, many of the faithful have been imbued with the Holy Spirit as well, giving them the power to continue to perform God's miracles throughout the earth.

Humankind: One of God's Greatest Miracles

For those who continue to believe that they have never been touched by a miracle, I would suggest that your miracle is no farther than a mirror away. You and the rest of the 7.6 billion people who currently inhabit Earth are truly miracles.[89] The human brain functions as the control system for the highly specialized body we human beings have been given. Over the course of a day, the semiautomatic human brain is able to process one million times more information than can be found within all of the world's books combined.[90] Many of these same books expound upon the awesome workings of the human body (of which only a scant few will be mentioned in this book).

According to Karin Lehnardt in her article "89 Amazing Human Body Facts," the following facts apply: The human body is made up of about 7 octillion atoms. Starting from the top down the following applies: The human brain contains 86 billion nerve cells joined by 100 trillion connections, and messages travel along these nerve cells as quickly as two hundred miles an hour. To achieve this feat the brain utilizes as much power as a ten-watt light bulb. We also find that over an average lifespan the heart beats more than 3 billion times, circulating blood about 12,000 miles a day, providing the necessary oxygen and nutrients to the more than 35 trillion cells within the body. Oxygen is acquired through the respiratory system, requiring the average person to breathe in the necessary oxygen at about 23,040 breaths a day—about 672,768,000 breaths over the course of an average lifetime. Meanwhile, the digestive system provides the necessary nutrients by processing about 100,000 pounds of food in a lifetime. No less amazing, within the human mouth, taste is detectable in as little as .0015 seconds. If we move to the eyes, we find that sight is just as awesome, as the human eye is able to distinguish between some 10 million colors. Regardless of the function of the body system, the majority of cells within all systems routinely regenerate themselves. For instance, the human skeleton will renew itself every ten years, while the top layer of skin will be replaced with new cells every thirty days.[91]

According to Kate Ng, only those cells of the inner lens of the eye, the muscle cells of the heart, and neurons of the cerebral cortex remain with a person throughout a lifetime.[92]

A Miracle Home

It stands to reason that in order to support something as complex and specialized as human life, a staggering number of conditions had to be met. The entire universe had to be fine-tuned in preparation for life as we know it. Aspects of that fine-tuning involved determining the size of planet Earth in relation to other planets, its rotational spin, as well as its position within our solar system. Another consideration was temperature gradient, as well as protection from the turbulence and violence of outer space.[93] In light of meeting those prerequisites, as well as many others as a result of the "Big Bang" explosion, English astronomer Sir Fred Hoyle states: "Creation produced the most precise and complex development of a Universe of astonishingly intricate designs that our scientists are only now discovering. The odds against our Universe, our Earth, and humanity itself occurring as a result of a chance explosion without a supernatural Designer are zero."[94]

The size of our planet is crucial because it determines the amount of gravitational pull. If Earth were larger, increased gravity would cause methane and ammonia gases to settle closer to our planet's surface.[95] In turn, if Earth were smaller and had less gravitational pull, then water, which is essential for life to exist, would dissipate into the atmosphere. Water is not only necessary for hydrating the human body, but its properties help to stabilize and moderate the air temperature in the atmosphere.[96] Planet rotation also has a tremendous effect upon life. The earth rotates once every twenty-four hours; if this rotation were even slightly slower, the temperature swings between night and day would reach extremes incompatible with human life. Should the earth's rotation quicken, the result would be a planet with inhospitable high winds, making human habitation difficult at best.[97]

The positioning of the planets within Earth's solar system also meets the conditions necessary to support human life. The moon is just the right size and distance to facilitate Earth's rotational axis. The earth's axis or tilt is directly responsible for the stabilization of temperatures and the change in seasons.[98] Even the planet Jupiter makes it possible for Earth to sustain life. The mammoth planet has 2.5 times more gravitational pull than Earth and is positioned like a defensive linebacker to deflect comets and space debris from pulverizing the earth's surface.[99]

Ironically, those comets that did manage to collide with earth were absolutely necessary for providing a significant amount of water to the earth's surface.[100] The moon collision with planet Earth proved the most essential as it increased the earth's size and gravitational pull, as well as the necessary repositioning of her axis. Both were modifications that proved absolutely essential for Earth's capacity to support life.[101]

The last prerequisite for life to consider is the presence of oxygen. Today Earth's atmosphere is made up of roughly 21 percent oxygen. It is believed that the oxygen levels on planet Earth increased following the growth of cyanobacteria, or blue-green algae plants. These plants survived through a process known as photosynthesis, in which sunshine, water, and carbon dioxide interact to produce both glucose and oxygen.[102]

A Beginning and a Good End

Whether Christians ascribe to the scientific understanding that the "Big Bang" created the universe or adhere to the literal text of the Bible, the good news is that this theory has brought science and religion into agreement that the universe had a beginning. If logic serves us well, every beginning requires a creator. According to scientists, the "Big Bang" explosion was just as precisely controlled and calculated by this creator as were all other events within the universe thereafter.[103] Mathematician John Carson Lennox states:

> The more we get to know about our universe, the more the hypothesis that there is a creator God, who destined the universe for a purpose, gains in credibility as the best explanation of why we are here.[104]

Every miracle I have written about has centered on humankind, God's prized creation. God's love for his prized creation need not be lost to us; all we need to do is think upon how we feel about anything we have created— our children, a work of art, an invention, or even a baked chocolate cake. Most of us value our creations beyond

measure and would like them to last forever (with the possible exception of the chocolate cake!). If we feel so strongly
for that which we have created, how much stronger does
the God of the Universe feel about us! The big difference
is that God loves better than we do, and only He has the
power to enable His creation to last forever. The Bible tells
us that all He asks in return is for us to believe in Him and
reciprocate His unabated love.

Chapter 8

The Infallible Word

Cry out for insight, and ask for understanding. Search for them as you would silver; seek them like hidden treasures. Then you will understand what it means to fear the LORD, and you will gain knowledge of God. (Proverbs 2:3–5)

*A*ll that you have read about life and death thus far supports the words of the Bible, a book Christians throughout the world recognize as the source of all truth. If you are grieving the loss of a precious loved one or facing your own immediate demise, please know that God has not forsaken you. Throughout the ages, God has left His handprint showing His involvement in our lives, knowing that at some point each and every one of us will be caught up in that suffocating chasm of grief. His presence is made evident throughout the Bible, through the resurrection of His only Son, as well as through revelations within science, and even NDEs and other miracles.

His earthly witnesses attest to these truths on a daily basis, all of which has everything to do with every tear you may weep and every anxious moment awaiting the death of a loved one or your own demise. Those who fervently seek out truth will find it, and that truth will help each and every one of us to better understand even life's hardest experiences through the eyes of our Heavenly Father.

It is common knowledge that the Bible is the bestselling book of all time. Estimates tell us that 100 million Bibles are printed each year, with 20 million sold in the United States alone.[105] You will never understand why this is so unless you begin reading its words yourself. Within its pages are countless verses pertaining to death and the promise of eternal life (a selection of many of those verses are presented in the Appendix of this book).

What Scripture Says—and Ways to Interpret It

According to the Bible, upon death the decedent's immortal spirit is separated from the decaying body, at which point the disembodied spirit is immediately ushered into Christ's presence. Those in Christ will remain with Him until His second coming to Earth, at which time the souls of both those in Christ and those who have rejected Christ will be reunited with their resurrected bodies and judged accordingly (2 Corinthians 5:8; Revelation 20:4–5).[106] A remnant of the Christian community interprets Holy Scripture as supportive of the belief in soul sleep (1 Corinthians 15:50–57), the belief that all the dead will sleep within their graves until the Lord's second coming, at which point all will be reunited with their resurrected bodies and judged. The bodies of those in Christ will be resurrected first, followed by the bodies of those in denial of Christ.[107] Both interpretations support the belief that the souls of all humans will live forever with their resurrected bodies in either heaven (with God) or hell (without God).[108]

It is not uncommon, when attempting to decipher Scripture, to find differing opinions amongst even the most learned theologians. It is best to keep in mind that although the Bible represents the Word of God and as such is infallible, the same cannot be said for human interpretations of Scripture.

As discussed in Chapter 5, there is a broad spectrum of opinions on whether or not NDEs should be considered biblically based. There are numerous accounts of individuals being brought back to life from death in the Bible (see 1 Kings 17:17–22; 2 Kings 4:32–35; 13:20–21; Matthew 27:50–53; 28:5–8; Mark 16:6; Luke 7:11–15; 8:41–42, 49–55; 24:5–6; John 11:1–44; Acts 9:36–41; 20:9–10). However, neither Lazarus nor any of the others in these passages are known to have returned with a revelation concerning the afterlife. Conversely, biblical writers—including Paul (2 Corinthians 12:2–5), John (the book of Revelation), and Daniel (Daniel 12:1–4)—have documented having seen visions of the afterlife. From all accounts none of these men had been returned from either clinical or biological death at the time of their vision.[109]

Despite the many skeptics, others within Christianity claim Scriptural support for NDEs. Episcopal priest John W. Price, in his book *Revealing Heaven,* mentions that Paul himself had a glimpse of heaven. In the third person (meaning Paul does not openly refer to himself), Paul states: "I know a man in Christ who fourteen years ago was caught up to the third heaven. Whether it was in the body or out of the body I do not know—God knows. And I know that this man . . . was caught up to paradise and heard inexpressible things, things that no one is permitted to tell" (2 Corinthians 12:2–4, NIV). Father Price also finds support for life after death as well as NDEs in 1 Corinthians 15:35–52, Daniel 12:1–3, Daniel 23:43, and Luke 16:19–31.[110] He suggests that Lazarus and the other souls who were brought back from death might have been reticent to reveal anything they possibly experienced while dead. Lastly, he refers to Jesus' words in John 10:16 as an explanation as to why people of other faiths experience heaven during their NDEs: "I have other sheep, too, that are not in this sheepfold. I must bring them also. They will listen to my voice, and there will be one flock with one shepherd."[111]

Reconciling NDEs with the Bible

Within the accounts of the multitude of individuals who have experienced NDEs, there is a consistent tapestry of events concerning heaven, which correlate closely with the scant biblical descriptions as to what the afterlife will be like: a sense of being disembodied, alteration in time and space, visualization of beautiful places and heavenly beings, judgment, and encountering an all-encompassing brilliant light that is often identified as Jesus. As John Burke describes in *Imagine Heaven*, many NDErs report that the city of God does not require any other means of light other than God Himself. Scripture says that *the Lamb (Jesus) is heaven's lamp* (Revelation 21:3).[112]

Overall, the majority of NDErs report having experienced an indescribable radiant light. Other NDEs are not as calming, such as Howard Storm's, whose experience was described in Chapter 5. He reports having to be rescued from the bowels of hell by a magnificent being of light. Beyond NDE reports, light itself remains a constant mystery even within the realm of science. Aspects of the connection of light with life as we know it will be discussed in the next chapter.

Another facet of NDEs that sometimes stymies even the person experiencing the NDE is the imparting of previous unknown knowledge. A very good example of this is Demi's NDE described in Jeffrey Long's *God and the Afterlife* and discussed at some length in Chapter 5. During her NDE, Demi (like many other individuals who have had this experience) was told that the most important thing in the universe is love. "And now these three remain: faith, hope, and love. But the greatest of these is love" (1 Corinthians 13:13, NIV). The next thing she was told puzzled her for many years. It was only after she randomly chose to watch a TV program about quantum physics that she understood why she was told she was exactly the same as everything in the universe, down to a single blade of grass.[113] As the program explained, only through the various deviations in the shape of quarks is it determined whether something develops into a plant, animal, or mineral.

I believe the point being made here reveals to Demi only part of the story—that all material visible to the human eye is perishable. This fact is supported in this biblical verse: "All flesh is like grass and all its glory like the flower of grass. The grass withers, and the flower falls" (1 Peter 1:24, ESV). This brings us right back to the relationship between quantum physics and many of the miracles mentioned in the Bible, cited in Chapter 7. These miracles, as well as the information imparted to Demi during her NDE, are more than likely representative of quantum physics at work through the hand of the Creator Himself. As such, no other area of science has helped us to better understand the connection between the visible and the invisible—something the Bible speaks of incessantly. And no other area of science has helped us to think smaller than small, down to the invisible parts of an atom, to the core of our being.

Reconciling Science with the Bible

Just as the Bible has continued to do for centuries, now quantum physics helps us reconnect with our Maker—just as other branches of science over the centuries, including medicine, archaeology, and cosmology, have substantiated biblical truths. In his book *The Signature of God,* Grant R. Jeffrey states, "there are no scientific errors found in the Bible's thousands of passages."[114] In light of the general consensus among biblical scholars that the earliest scriptures of the Old Testament were written between 1446–1406 BC, the only plausible explanation for its insightful accuracy is that the Bible was inspired by the one and only God of creation.

Medicine

When you consider that the ancient people of Israel had no electron microscopes or any other means of observing pathogens, it is amazing that Scripture teaches its readers to follow the first rule of medical asepsis—washing with clean water. Scripture also expounds upon the benefits of sunlight and prescribed the quarantine of the sick, including those with leprosy. Even more amazing is the recommendation that male infants be circumcised on the eighth day following their birth.

Centuries later, medical science determined that the blood-clotting chemical prothrombin peaks to its highest level at eight days after a child's birth. Dietary restrictions in the Bible also reflect an uncanny understanding, including the avoidance of excessive fat intake within the diet. Today we know that high levels of cholesterol and triglycerides, stemming from a fatty diet, will cause plaque formation within the arteries that can lead to death.[115] Medical science leaves very little doubt that God was looking out for His chosen people and for anyone else who would trust Him.

Archaeology

Over the course of the past 175 years, many of the great archaeological minds have also been left convinced of the authenticity of Scripture. Without exception they conclude that the time period between events in Christ's life and the writing of Scripture recounting those events was too slight to permit any misrepresentation of what had occurred. In addition, they determined that the apostles were indeed the genuine writers of the New Testament and that their description of the fulfillment of all seventeen messianic prophecies through Jesus Christ was accurate, defying the laws of probability.[116]

Archaeology speaks to the authenticity of not just the New Testament but the Old Testament as well. A good example of how Scripture and science support one another involves excavations of Jericho undertaken by Professor John Garstang in 1930 and 1936. In the quest to understand what had transpired during the conquest of the Promised Land, excavations revealed an irrefutable fact stated in the Bible—the city walls of Jericho fell outward, rather than having an expected inward descent. This gave the attackers a keen advantage in that they would have been able to climb through the rubble and capture the city. For those who worked on the excavation, it became clear that "only the supernatural power of God could have caused the city's walls to fall outwards."[117] The biblical account of the event states, "The wall fell down flat, so that the people went up into the city, every man straight before him, and they captured the city" (Joshua 6:20, ESV).

A more recent archeological discovery in 2009 uncovered ancient Egyptian coins bearing the image of Joseph—the same biblical Joseph whose father Jacob had given his son the enviable coat of many colors. Soon after receiving the coat, young Joseph's ten older brothers sold him into slavery. Years later the brothers would reunite, only to learn that Joseph had risen to a high place within the Egyptian pharaoh's court (Genesis 37–50).[118] In light of all that has been unearthed throughout the centuries, as Dr. Nelson Glueck states in his book *Rivers in the Desert*, "no archaeological discovery has ever controverted a Biblical reference."[119]

Cosmology and the Law of Thermodynamics

Cosmology, a branch of astronomy, is the study of the origin and development of the universe. It attempts to answer questions involving the origin and evolution of all there is that makes up the vastness of outer space. In 1964, with the overall scientific acceptance of the Big Bang theory, a large gap between science and biblical Scripture had finally been bridged. Science no longer had grounds to disagree with Scripture in respect to whether the universe and Earth had a beginning—whether or not it materialized out of nothing, or (according to the more current opinion) that "nothing" actually holds *quantum fields and virtual particles*. Either way, both science and the Bible concur that *nothing comes from nothing*. If you choose to take logic seriously, it stands to reason that in order to create something from nothing or even from quantum fields and particles, there needs to be a Creator behind the scene.[120]

Science and the Bible also stand together in support of the law of entropy, a bylaw of thermodynamics. Entropy in respect to the universe means everything is running down or running out of energy, toward a point in time when it will cease to exist. Science and the Bible come together once again in the description of both planet Earth and the universe *as chaotic*—full of contradictions, surprises, and possibilities, as well as predictions for an unavoidable *apocalyptic end.*[121] Should this be the case, the truth is blatantly clear that science of itself has neither the tools, power, nor authority to change the predicted course of events, nor is it able to offer humankind a palatable option to its own demise.

Perhaps our hope lies within the words written in an ancient book—a book so often left on the shelf, dusty and unread. Should we dare open its pages maybe, just maybe, *the truth will set us free* (John 8:32). I believe that scientist and Anglican priest John Polkinghorne, in his book *Quantum Physics and Theology,* gives us the right recipe for the human dilemma: Both science and theology have always strived for the same end, *truth.* In so doing, they have even adopted a similar paradigm for reaching that truth.[122]

Dr. Michael Guillen expounds on this in his book *Amazing Truths: How Science and the Bible Agree.* At their inception, Guillen explains, both science and religion shared a cyclical or circular worldview, in that everything was seen as repeating itself, having neither a beginning nor an end. Both Eastern religion and to some extent Judaism were based upon a cyclical worldview. It was through the Christian Bible that science eventually derived its leaning toward a linear time approach in which "everything in the universe participates interactively in a universal story line."[123]

Science and theology have historically continued to build upon past revelations within each of their domains. For instance, just as the Christian Messiah fulfilled messianic Jewish prophecy, so great minds in science including Galileo, Newton, Lorenz, and Einstein paved the way for the advent of the Big Bang theory as well as the astounding world of quantum physics.

Beyond Science

Science has come as close to truth as it possibly can. Through means of the scientific method—formulating hypotheses that have either been substantiated or refuted through repeated observation and experimentation—science has reached its own best logical conclusions. The scientific method has served science well—to a point.

If you consider Gödel's incompleteness theory and Heisenberg's uncertainty principle, even science admits to falling short of absolute infallibility. With the realization that 95 percent of what there is to know about our world remains hidden from us, you cannot help but wonder if logic alone will lead the way to truth.[124]

On the other hand, the main purpose of the Bible is the revelation of the one true God, as well as serving as a tutorial on how we are to live in this world in preparation for being with God in eternity. It does not take long to realize that Scripture was never meant to be a science book, and that many questions pertaining to the universe, ourselves, our Creator, death, and eternity will likely remain unanswered this side of the veil.

Meanwhile, the time wasted believing that science and theology are in some way adversarial has failed to serve mankind well. The surest path to truth will always lie within a strong alliance between logic, intuition, and faith.[125] As Dr. Michael Guillen states: "Together science and the Bible will enable us to see in the dark as we journey toward the light."[126]

The last four chapters of our journey bring us to the heart of the matter, without which a book pertaining to death and eternity could not be written in truth.

Chapter 9

Our Father

See how very much our Father loves us, for he calls us his children, and that is what we are! (1 John 3:1)

*S*cripture speaks volumes of the great love God has for humankind. Knowing full well that His love for us lies well beyond our comprehension, the Bible serves as a linear story line of that love from the creation of the universe and planet Earth, to humankind's creation, and lastly our redemption from sin through God incarnate, Jesus Christ. "There is no greater love than to lay down one's life for one's friends" (John 15:13).

To the extent that God prized His creation, particularly humankind, it becomes abundantly clear that our existence was never an accident. Throughout Scripture, God reveals His long-term plans for His prized creation, explaining the extent of His efforts to prepare a habitable home for us on planet Earth. Science calculates that the earth is about 4.5 billion years old, and it is believed that *Homo sapiens* appeared on the scene as recently as 50,000 years ago.[127] Christian creationists stand by biblical scholars who, through the recording of biblical lifespans, as well as measuring the amount of time between events, have determined that both the creation of the earth and the appearance of humankind on the planet occurred only six thousand years ago.[128] Though scientists and creationists differ on their opinion of the age of Earth as well as when and how mankind came to inhabit the planet, they concur as to the uniqueness of humankind in comparison with other forms of life.

The Intricacy of the Human Brain

As discussed in Chapter 7, there is no doubt that the human body is a marvel within itself, especially the human brain. For instance, the manmade computer Titan has some 10 billion network connections requiring 8.4 megawatts of electricity to run, compared to the human brain's 125 trillion connections operating on a mere 1,800 calories per day. Though the computer is able to accomplish many things faster than the human brain, such as performing specific tasks and calculations, it is yet to be developed to the point that it is able to multitask the way the human brain can. While on automatic pilot our brains enable us to perpetually multitask: breathing, thinking, talking, tasting, listening, seeing, touching, walking, smelling, and such, more often than not done simultaneously.

Our indispensable computer rests neatly within our cranium, while its manmade counterpart requires significantly more storage space.[129] Most of us are quick to acknowledge that the present-day computer came about over the course of the past eight decades through the comprehensive work of highly intelligent computer engineers. Ironically, so many of us have difficulty acknowledging that we, not unlike our desk or laptop computer, were created by a far more advanced intelligence than our own.

Yes, God created every microscopic aspect of each and every one of us, including our amazing brain. He alone gave us our very own customized brain, by which we are able to express our creativity as well as speak intelligently. The brain remains the seat of our moral compass, compelling us to honor and respect both the living and the dead. Consequently, we are the only mammal known to give its dead an honorable burial and/or cremation.

The fact that we were created by Almighty God becomes even more apparent when we consider our innate knowledge of His sovereignty as well as the eternity awaiting us through Him.[130] "He has planted eternity in the human heart" (Ecclesiastes 3:11). Being a relational God, from the moment of our creation to the present day, God's entanglement within every aspect of our being has not waned. He is there in our living and our dying—and if we so choose, our eternity.

God's Entanglement with Humankind

Merriam-Webster defines the word "entanglement" as "the condition of being deeply involved." As discussed in Chapter 6, when a proton divides into two separate identical protons, even when distanced from one another, there remains an ongoing communication between the two individual protons. This communication is instantaneous, ten times faster than the speed of light. The unending interaction continues regardless how far apart the protons might become.[131] The more I read about entanglement, the more it reminds me of God's relationship with humankind, as witnessed through His unrelenting love for us and the way in which He inspires us to love one another.

God's brand of unfaltering love and His entanglement with us brings to mind true stories pertaining to what is sometimes referred to as the *sixth sense*. The sixth sense has been known to surface at times as a vague uneasy feeling in a person's gut concerning a loved one distanced from him or her; more often than not, the person learns that the foreboding was warranted.

Just as we feel our loved one's pain, whether near or far, God feels ours as well. He knows everything that befalls us. Though in this life the reasons He may not change our circumstances are often unclear to us, if we allow Him, He always uses our pain for the betterment of all concerned. The Bible tells us, "our present troubles are small and won't last very long. Yet they produce for us a glory that vastly outweighs them and will last forever!" (2 Corinthians 4:17).

Down to the very smallest molecule of our being, God remains entangled with us through the good times and the bad. True to His great love for us, He will never move on to an easier project; rather, He promises, "Be strong and courageous. Do not be afraid or terrified because of them, for the LORD your God goes with you; he will never leave you nor forsake you" (Deuteronomy 31:6, NIV). Disentanglement from God will always be our choice alone.

Moving toward the Light

An important aspect of God's entanglement with humankind involves light. Perhaps the word "light" immediately brings to mind the sunshine, a provision God gave us when He decreed, "Let there be light" (Genesis 1:3). God understood how important the sun would be to our very survival on planet Earth. In our material world, the sun's light is nothing more than a substitute for the luminous light of God. Our relationship to His light goes well beyond the wonderful sunshine available to us on our earthly home. When God refers to light in the Bible, He is referring to His very personage, as well as to His word. He does not mean to suggest that He is but one of many light sources, but rather that He alone is the only one true light.

When Jesus said, "I am the light of the world. If you follow me, you won't have to walk in darkness, because you will have the light that leads to life" (John 8:12), He was not saying that He was the sunshine of this world but rather that He and the invisible God are one. As such, Jesus alone serves as the light of life. Both science and the Bible attest to the uniqueness of light. Light is known to be timeless, inhabiting a realm where the past, present, and future coexist. Even more mind-boggling is the fact that light and matter are interchangeable—giving a scientific bent to both God's incarnation through Jesus and Jesus' resurrection.[132]

God tells us that He "created human beings in His own image . . . male and female he created them" (Genesis 1:27). To that extent, we too were derived from the light. Once again, through both science and the Bible we understand that ordinary matter, including flesh and blood, can be transformed into luminous light or energy. For that to occur in the case of flesh and blood, the body must die.[133] Not only must the body die, but man's sinful nature must die before he is made ready to reunite with the heavenly Father.

When God says He is the light, He also states that "there is no darkness in him at all" (1 John 1:5). Darkness is often a metaphor for sin. That being the case, it is clear that God is absolutely incompatible with sin. Each and every one of us must be cleansed of our sin to render us acceptable to reunite with our Maker. Christians believe that the cleansing of our human sinful nature is only possible through a belief in Jesus Christ who through His crucifixion and resurrection became the necessary atonement to God for humankind's sin. As such, Jesus Christ as part of the Holy Trinity has been declared both the truth and the Word: "You were cleansed from your sins when you obeyed the truth, so now you must show sincere love to each other as brothers and sisters. Love each other deeply with all your heart. For you have been born again, but not to a life that will quickly end. Your new life will last forever because it comes from the eternal living word of God" (1 Peter 1:22–23).

In light of all that has been revealed to us, it comes as little surprise that those on their deathbeds often report seeing a bright light immediately before taking their last breath. Nor is it surprising that the majority of NDE survivors report having seen an indescribably bright light as they slipped from this world. Hallucinations? I think not—rather, once again a testimony to God's abiding love, a love that has fought for us and died for us.

Short of removing our free will, God has taken every conceivable action in order to bring us home to Him. Remember that God loves you beyond your human comprehension and that you need not fear death. You merely have to follow God's light within this realm into the next.

Chapter 10

Full Circle

The LORD cares deeply when his loved ones die.
(Psalm 116:15)

*L*et's turn at last to our own personal big pictures—
the ones even we can't see. At present, in our mortal
state, there remains (in quantum terms) a non-local
connection between us and God.[134] "I can never escape
from your Spirit! I can never get away from your presence!"
(Psalm 139:7). Mindful that we are of the same Maker,
and that the same intrinsic connection we all hold with our
heavenly Father exists between each of us as well, is it not
true that every kindness enriches each and every human
heart, while at the same time every hurt wounds us all?
Similarly, it is not unlikely that each deed great or small
contributes to the ongoing duel between cosmic goodness
and evil that permeates God's universe.

Only after we die will God assess what impact we have made in our individual lives. Even after death we continue to impact the lives of those who knew us in this life, who will either weep or rejoice at our passing. Should they weep, the Bible tells us that those who mourn the death of a loved one are blessed. "Blessed are those who mourn, for they will be comforted" (Matthew 5:4, NIV). If you have ever mourned the passing of a loved one, you probably did not feel especially blessed at that time, and perhaps nothing was able to truly comfort you. Still, there is great truth in Jesus' words. Having the capacity to love another, if only a fraction of the way in which Christ loves us, is indeed a blessing.

When a loved one returns to the Father, the more they were loved, the greater our pain. But that pain is a miniscule trade-off when you consider the alternative of never having had the opportunity to love that individual in this life. As for comfort, that will certainly come to pass if you will trustingly place yourself and your deceased loved one in the care of the Lord God.

Dealing with the Anxiety of Death

God never wanted or expected us to take death lightly—either our own, that of a loved one, or even the deaths of strangers we learn of through mass media. Biblical history certainly suggests that within the scheme of things God himself thought death a "big deal." In the beginning, all Adam and Eve had to do for God to continue to provide for their needs and ensure their immortality was to obey His edict not to eat of the tree of knowledge. Most of us know what happened, and to this day all humans and animals have suffered the consequences.

Noted psychiatrist and humanitarian Dr. Elizabeth Kubler-Ross dedicated much of her medical practice to working with terminally ill patients and learning what transpires during the dying process. Now deceased herself, her legacy includes an in-depth description of the psychological stages a dying patient experiences when facing imminent death:

Stage 1—denial and isolation;

Stage 2—anger;

Stage 3—bargaining;

Stage 4—depression; and

Stage 5—acceptance.[135]

Though Dr. Kubler-Ross's book *On Death and Dying* was published in 1969, her five-stage model continues to be used to help patients and those in the helping professions to better understand the process of dying in terms of change management. Some practitioners in the change management field have criticized the five-stage model for being too simplistic; they feel it does not account for the broad spectrum of emotions experienced by those going through a significant change in their lives.[136]

Dr. Kubler-Ross explains that fear of death is universal. Every person's unconscious mind is unable to perceive its own death, though it does perceive its own immortality.[137] In Chapter 3 we touched on humankind's innate belief in its immortality. Unfortunately, over the past several decades the fear of death has been significantly exacerbated within Western culture due to two major changes.

The first change is to the medical paradigm, which often focuses upon prolonging human life at all costs. In many instances, when this is the main focus, it often proves to be a detriment to the patient's quality of life as well as his or her quality of dying.[138] Living in this twenty-first century, a peaceful death at home surrounded by one's loved ones is no longer the norm. More likely, the scene unfolds in a hospital room, where the dying patient is found to be overmedicated and kept alive by a network of tubes, blinking lights, and bleeping computers. At the same time, an army of well-meaning staff flutter about, conscientiously working toward any other end *except* the patient's peaceful death.

The Cause of Our Anxiety

While advancements in medical technology have most definitely contributed to humankind's death anxiety, I believe another change is the primary contributor—the Western world's estrangement from God. It would seem inevitable that when a people stops believing in God and His promise of life after death through Jesus Christ, death anxiety increases, and the race to live forever in decaying bodies seems the last hope. More than six decades ago Dr. Kubler-Ross commented on the shift away from religion as being correlational with an increase in death anxiety: "religion gives hope and purpose when dealing with painful occurrences in this life, and society has not offered a viable substitute."[139]

In fact, many studies in the fields of psychiatry, mental health, behavioral sciences, medical sciences, and religious studies have focused on the correlation between religiosity and death anxiety. A significant number of these studies conclude that the more religious a person is, the less anxious he or she is about death. This is attributable to the religious teaching that life continues beyond the grave. Other studies have found that religiosity can actually increase death anxiety due to the fear of judgment in the next life. Still other studies have concluded that a correlation between religiosity and fear of death is nonexistent.[140]

Regardless of these findings, human beings will always attempt psychologically to protect themselves against the prospect of dying. In a play to cheat death, a percentage of the population will challenge their own mortality through living on the edge—for example, driving recklessly or participating in other dangerous activities—which needless to say never works.[141]

Suicide is never the Answer

Tragically, over the past few decades the number of people willfully taking their own lives has also increased dramatically. CDC statistics show that US suicide rates increased as much as 28 percent from 1999 through 2017. Today it is the second leading cause of death for Americans between the ages of ten through thirty-four, and the fourth leading cause for those between ages thirty-five and fifty-four.[142]

Suicide is not so much a fear of dying as it is a fear of living within whatever seemingly untenable circumstances people might find themselves. Often suicide is directly related to mental illness and substance abuse. Both the pain that precipitates this desperate act and the pain left in its wake are almost incomprehensible. When a person takes his own life, loved ones are often left with not only the pain of their loss but a nagging sense of guilt that they did not do more to prevent the tragedy.

In Christian families, in particular, there is often great consternation that a loved one lost to suicide will remain separated from God throughout eternity. The truth is that Scripture does not support this, for nowhere does it state that those who take their own lives are eternally separated from God. Nonetheless it is true that suicide is a sin against God, as the human body is a temple of God Himself and is to be honored as such. We were created in God's own image and are not to murder ourselves or anyone else.

A Better Way to Give Up a Life

While God does not want us to throw our precious lives away in the senseless act of suicide, He does want us to give our lives away on His behalf, in senseless acts of love. "If you cling to your life, you will lose it; but if you give up your life for me, you will find it" (Matthew 10:39). We were all born with the purpose of fulfilling the plans God has for each and every one of us in this life. Scripture attests to the fact that God never stops working in and through our lives. Even unto death no one need be lost, even those who die through a suicidal act of myopic hopelessness.

We are told that when our Lord and Savior shed His blood on the cross, He did so in order that the sins of all mankind past, present, and future would be forgiven. All that is required on our part is to accept Jesus Christ's selfless gift. If the suicide victim accepted that gift prior to his or her passing, according to the Bible he now rests with the Lord:

> And I am convinced that nothing can ever sepa-
> rate us from God's love. Neither death nor life,
> neither angels nor demons, neither fears for today
> nor our worries about tomorrow—not even the
> powers of hell can separate us from God's love. No
> power in the sky above or in the earth below—
> indeed, nothing in all creation will ever be able to
> separate us from the love of God that is revealed
> in Christ Jesus our Lord. (Romans 8:38–39)

Is it not so that the invisible God, through the short life of His beloved Son Jesus Christ, showed us all the love, hope, and empathy meant to carry us through this life to the next?

In his book *Empathy: Love and Life beyond Self*, Christian life coach Kenneth E. Rupert gives us a working definition for empathy: "Empathy begins when you voluntarily set aside your standing, status, or station, to enter into someone else's reality in order to be a catalyst for that person's restoration."[143] More than any time in our lives, when we or a loved one lay dying, we need and deserve love and empathy from those tending to our physical, emotional, and spiritual needs. Often, the inability to face death, either one's own or someone else's, renders a person impotent to accept or provide the emotional support so very much needed at such a time. Unfortunately, denial never changes the reality of death. Instead, denial stifles our ability to emulate Christ's empathy for the benefit of another and prevents us from accepting it for ourselves.

Rather than relying on your own understanding, go to the Lord for your strength, and accept His empathy. In God's time we all must die a physical death, in order that we might be reunited with our Maker. Physical death remains nonnegotiable until that time when our Lord God returns to this earth and removes the thorn of death from our flesh. Until then, our best course of action is to live our life right with God, so that when death touches us, we will remain assured that we will continue life throughout eternity with Him.

Chapter 11

It's Your Choice

Look! I stand at the door and knock. If you hear my voice and open the door, I will come in, and we will share a meal together as friends. (Revelation 3:20)

*L*et me begin by clarifying what being a Christian means to me personally. Initially, it means to believe in Jesus Christ as the incarnate God. It is to acknowledge that He alone is the Creator and the force behind all that we see, as well as all that we do not see in the universe. It is a belief that Jesus Christ died and was resurrected so that the sins of all those who have ever lived might be forgiven. To receive God's grace, all we are required to do is repent and believe on Christ. If our belief is sincere, our lives will be changed, and at the very least we will attempt to emulate Christ's love through all we say and do within this life.

While I believe it is good to be a part of a Christian church community, I do not ascribe to the position that Jesus Christ is represented exclusively through any one of the 43,000 Christian denominations in the world (as of 2012).[144] Many Christians affiliated with these Christian denominations share my sentiments. The position that no single denomination is exclusively representative of God's Word was articulated by world-renowned apologist C. S. Lewis, who wrote in his book *Mere Christianity*: "The central belief of Christianity is that Christ's death has somehow put us right with God and given us a fresh start. A good many different theories have been held as to how it works; what all Christians are agreed on is that it does work."[145]

Despite the fact that much of the Western Hemisphere has been secularized since Lewis published his insightful book in 1942, Christianity remains the largest religious group, numbering 2.45 billion adherents worldwide.[146] Though this number speaks volumes, I prefer to speak of Christianity as a faith rather than a religion because religion is for the most part a human creation, whereas faith comes from God and as such is directed back to Him alone.

If all of the above is even remotely true, then the Christian faith should be every person's faith—and so it was meant to be. The next logical question is: Why has the faith continued to be denied by so many, beginning with Adam and Eve within God's paradise on earth?

It would probably take several volumes to fully answer that question. I will attempt to give you a cursory look at some of the more likely reasons people choose to turn away from the innate truth within them. In doing so, I will refer throughout this chapter to the words of pastor and contemporary apologist Dr. Timothy Keller. Much of what Keller discusses in his book *The Reason for God* references Lewis's classic work, as well as Keller's own personal experiences working with young skeptics in Manhattan.

Reasons for Unbelief

Exclusivity

The first and foremost problem many people have with the Christian faith is its exclusive claims in respect to God's truth. I will concede that the Christian faith is an all-or-nothing faith. For instance, you must believe everything in the Bible, is recognized as the Word of God. As such, God is either true in every way He presents Himself or He is a liar and not God at all. As discussed in Chapter 8, the Bible's authenticity has been proven in numerous ways, one of which is through the fulfillment of many detailed prophecies throughout history to our present age.[147] The Christian God is a proven God, a God who invites all to His embrace. Through the followers of Jesus Christ, God incarnate, the poor have been fed, the blind have been led, the grief-stricken have been comforted, and even God's enemies have been forgiven at their request. Through Jesus Christ men have seen God, empowering them to reject their own nature and enabling them to perform acts of mercy in His name.

Based on the assumption that God is unknowable, or different from the way in which He is depicted in Holy Scripture, skeptics often challenge Christianity's claim to a superior knowledge of spiritual reality. Keller asks nonbelievers to show him proof there is no God, or that God is somehow different from the way in which Holy Scripture portrays Him. Of course, proof is never provided because it does not exist. From this premise, Keller concludes that if it is narrow to believe in the exclusive God of Christianity, it is no less exclusive or narrow to believe that the one true God does not exist, or that He is not who He says He is.

Realistically, we all have a worldview that we cling to, and most worldviews are far more difficult to prove than the Christian worldview. The only logical conclusion that remains is that lack of faith is no less a faith than faith itself.[148]

Evil and Suffering

Another common complaint against Christianity is the presence of evil and suffering in our world. Death itself is associated with sin and evil, and as such can sometimes become an obstacle to the belief in a loving God. The perpetuation of evil through either natural or unnatural acts or events leads many of us to cry out with the resounding question "Why?"

In the face of evil a person's faith is often pushed to its very limits, and if we rely on our own limited understanding then belief in a loving God can be difficult to say the least. Those experiencing life's challenges without faith in

God often become alienated and bristle at so much as the mention of God. For others, life's challenges serve as a catalyst to bring them back into the fold. The Bible cautions us, when experiencing life's difficulties, to "Trust in the LORD with all your heart; do not depend on your own understanding. Seek his will in all you do, and he will show you which path to take" (Proverbs 3:5–6).

A question often asked is how a loving God can just sit back and let bad things happen to both good and bad people alike. Though God does not cause evil to enter our lives, He does not necessarily spare us from experiencing evil either, though He always gives us the opportunity to weigh in on the side of goodness. From my personal experience, I believe that if we cooperate with God, in His infinite wisdom He uses all evil to bring us back to Him. Pastor Keller takes what C. S. Lewis professes as true, a step further when he states that *evil and suffering may, in fact, be evidence for God.* He points out that within the natural world there exist all those things that people fear and retreat from—disease, death, destruction, and oppression—and thus such things are considered *perfectly natural.* When the etiology of bad things is of the natural world, they fail to offend us in the same way they do when we bring God into the picture. We expect that a loving God would be fair and just with us—giving speculation to the probability that our own innate sense of justice comes from the very God we often turn away from.[149] With God or without His presence in the natural world, sin exists along with all those things we prefer to avoid, and in the end it is only God who is able to usher us back to His sinless world.

The Sins of the Church

Another stumbling block that prevents many people from committing their lives to Christ is a belief that the church is responsible for much of the injustice in the world. Realistically, the church was not established to benefit the saints but for those who are sick in spirit. Christians are not perfect people, and sometimes we do things both as a corporate body and as individuals that do not reflect the God whom we profess to worship. In addition, Christians are not saved through their works but through God's grace, although it is certainly expected that those who claim to be Christians will follow through with good works. Professing believers who continually fail in this regard will give cause to question whether they are really committed to all that the Christian faith stands for.

An unbiased assessment of the good dispersed through the Christian church down through the ages will show that it has continued to be a champion of humanitarian causes throughout the world. Examples of but a few of the Christian organizations at work within the world today include Caritas International, Emmaus International, Lutheran World Relief, United Methodist Committee on Relief, The International Justice Mission, Food for the Hungry, Prison Fellowship International, Samaritan's Purse, Mercy Ships, and World Vision International.[150]

In addition, countless Christians throughout history have forfeited their freedom and even their lives for the sake of their faith and the well-being of all humanity. Many clergymen and prominent Christians have endured imprisonment and even death for promoting civil rights in opposition to government oppression—again, to name but a few: Dietrich Bonhoeffer, Martin Luther King, Desmond Tutu, William Wilberforce, and John Woolman.[151]

Let us also recognize that other religious groups, as well as those who subscribe to a secular worldview, are no less guilty of perpetuating injustice and violence in this world than are wayward Christians. The reality of the situation is that evil often prevails over goodness— and will continue to do so, until Jesus returns to this earth. In the meantime, humankind remains ensnared within a web of spiritual warfare that has ensued well beyond creation. We alone are on the frontlines of that war, and only we can choose where our allegiance lies.

God, the Wisest Choice

Some believe that no individual of any intelligence could ever believe in God, much less all the amazing truths about God recorded in the Bible. Actually, this assumption could not be further from the truth. Most of the pioneers whose research and analyses have discovered and formulated the laws and concepts that are the basis for modern scientific research were practicing Christians. The list is long and includes such notables as Bacon, Newton, Pasteur, Linnaeus, Faraday, Pascal, Lord Kelvin, Maxwell, and Kepler.[152]

In response to this impressive list of Christian notables, the skeptic might shrug his/her shoulders, glibly dismissing this fact through reasoning that these men lived in an era when everyone was brainwashed into believing the same preposterous nonsense. This presumption does not stand, however, because 65.4% of Nobel Prize Laureates between 1901 and 2000 identified with various forms of the Christian faith. Furthermore, Christians have won a total of 78.3% of all the Nobel Prizes awarded within this contemporary time frame. It is no less impressive to review the percentage of prizes awarded to Christians within each given field of expertise: 72.5% in Chemistry, 65.3% in Physics, 62% in Medicine, 54% in Economics, and 49.5% in Literature.[153]

That said, intelligence (or high IQ) is not a prerequisite for faith. While God-given intelligence lends itself to the use of logic in the search for truth, it sometimes leads to pride and arrogance, even to the point of replacing God with oneself. Finally, logic within itself, without intuition and the faith that truth even exists, is not powerful enough to deliver us to the truth of this world or the next.[154] This being the case, it is those who search with the innocence of a small child—no matter how high or low their intelligence—who will find the truth of God before all others.

Jesus Christ said, "you will know the truth, and the truth will set you free" (John 8:32). The Christian places his faith in the words of Jesus Christ and Holy Scripture, both of which are held to be infallible. Reaching that truth rarely comes easy; the road, more often than not, is bumpy with many twists and turns. In order to even begin a quest for the truth, you must have a modicum of confidence—or if you like, faith—that truth is something that can be found.

People will employ various strategies as a means of discovering God and His truth. While the cognitive road to God is a road much traveled, and an excellent way in which to begin your quest, in and of itself it will never carry you to your destination. The Christian faith is so much more than merely a cognitive exercise. In fact, if you end your search in a book you may find yourself little more than a Pharisee. Faith will never reach its fruition on the pages of a book, not even the Holy Bible. Faith, much like love, must be lived, practiced, and shared on a daily basis. It is a dichotomy of logic and mysticism and must be shared so that it leaves its mark upon every person it touches. Faith is on a continuum, and even the faithful will at times find it to be particularly elusive. When that occurs, and it surely will, *keep knocking and the door will be opened unto you,* over and over again.

Once you glimpse the Christian truth, hold onto your new faith tightly, live your life in accordance with Holy Scripture, and choose wisely in all things. Even with faith, and sometimes because of it, you will experience the problems and pain of this world—and yes, death and grieving. But you will never lose that quiet joy that comes with the knowledge that beyond the grave, you are promised an eternity with your heavenly Father.

Chapter 12

It Is Finished!

It is finished! I am the Alpha and the Omega—
the Beginning and the End. To all who are thirsty
I will give freely from the springs of the water of
life. All who are victorious will inherit all these
blessings, and I will be their God, and they will
be my children. (Revelation 21:6–7)

It is finished! These were the last three words Jesus
Christ uttered as He hung dying upon the cross of
Calvary. Have you ever stopped to think what meaning those three words hold for all humanity, including us?
At first glance the meaning appears to clearly express Jesus'
release to death following six hours of interminable suffering upon the cross. Of course it was finished, and it
would seem that Jesus was just proclaiming the inevitable.
After looking harder and longer, however, you will find
that Jesus' seemingly straightforward words go well beyond

their initial interpretation and in fact are but the beginning of His story.

Today we have the advantage of those who went before us, often giving their very lives as witness to what Jesus meant when He cried out those words. Jesus was proclaiming that the God of the universe had successfully completed His mission here on Earth—that through His death on the cross all humankind was once again made acceptable in the eyes of God. Jesus' blood alone had atoned for the sins of us all, and through Him we are made dead to our sins and are raised to everlasting life. Jesus' death and resurrection did for us what we could not do for ourselves.

Simply put, without Jesus' sacrificial death we could never again be reunited with God and be a part of His holy sinless kingdom—just as the healthy cells of the human body cannot coexist with a diseased cancerous cell, as one diseased cell promises the destruction of all the healthy cells that God originally created within us. All disease and death are a result of sin—and every human being, without exception, will succumb to that sin on this earth unless they partake in the lifesaving, purifying serum of Jesus' holy blood.

Jesus Christ's sacrificial love offering of Himself, followed by His miraculous resurrection from the dead at the will of the Holy Father, is the very core of the Christian faith. Through the personage of Jesus, the concept of the triune God—God the Father, Jesus Christ the Son, and the Holy Spirit—was revealed to all humanity. For the Jewish people, the concept of God being considered a part of three identifiable entities was nothing short of blasphemy.

Despite this strong objection, the overwhelming evidence that this was indeed the case caused many Jews to break rank with Jewish tradition and follow the living God. Still others remained skeptical, as people from all creeds continue to be to this day. It would appear that the human heart has changed little from what it was two thousand years ago when Jesus walked this earth.

For many, the truth preached by Jesus continues to appear too good to be true. Timothy Keller attests to this statement as he claims that one of the more common objections to Christianity is that what the Bible proclaims about Jesus and the resurrection is nothing more than wishful thinking, a pie-in-the-sky hope that death is not our last stop.[155] Skeptics continue to stand strong in their refusal to be "duped" into believing that storybook endings really do happen. Jesus Christ's very existence on planet Earth has often been questioned, and more so that He was crucified and resurrected.

One Skeptic's Search

One of those former skeptics, Lee Strobel, a respected and well-known legal affairs journalist, took matters into his own hands and conducted a painstaking investigation into the truth concerning Jesus Christ's life, death, and resurrection. At the end of that search he concluded that the overwhelming historical, archaeological, documentary, and medical evidence all attest to the fact that Jesus walked this earth within the time frame the Bible documents, and that He was all that He claimed to be.

For the purposes of this book, further discussion will be limited to Lee Strobel's findings concerning Christ's death and resurrection. In his book *The Case for Christ,* Strobel presents solid proof of Christ's death on the cross as well as His resurrection three days after.

Operating on the premise of medical forensics that dead bodies do tell tales, Strobel began his search. Two major hurdles to be overcome in Jesus' case were the facts that His death had occurred two millennia ago and that there had never been a body to examine. Still, the documented description of the pain and suffering Jesus endured before and after being nailed to the cross continues to reveal the truth of His death and resurrection to the present day. With that understanding, Strobel engaged Doctor Alexander Metherell, who over the years had put his numerous talents to work to uncover the extent to which our Savior suffered and eventually died on that Roman cross. Strobel pointedly posed his questions as follows: "What actually happened at the crucifixion? What was Jesus' cause of death? Is there any possible way he could have survived this ordeal?"[156]

Dr. Metherell gives the following account as to what Jesus would have been subjected to both prior to and during His crucifixion: Roman crucifixion was by no means devised to be something anyone could walk away from; rather, it followed grisly and brutal steps that were meant to deliver a slow and tortuous death. In Jesus' case, He had been flogged at least thirty-nine times from the shoulders down to the back of His legs. When the whipping was completed, the shredded skin would have exposed the veins, muscles, and even the bowels of the victim. In Jesus' case, though He survived the beating He would have been in a critical state of hypovolemic shock due to extensive blood loss, which in and of itself could cause death. Scripture supports this when referring to His being unable to support the weight of the heavy wooden cross He was forced to carry on the road to Calvary. With the help of Simon of Cyrene, Jesus reached His destination, and the brutality continued.

In summary of that brutality: Spikes were driven into the median nerves of His wrists and the nerves of His feet, causing excruciating pain. The effects of hanging on the cross for six hours would have dislocated both shoulders. Additional pain would have been endured with every breath, as the legs would have to be drawn up against the inserted nails in the feet in order to exhale. In the end, the crucified victim would die a slow death of asphyxiation. Lastly, the *coup de grace* in Jesus' case would have been the sword that was thrust into His right side, puncturing the heart. Clinically speaking, it would be absolutely impossible for Jesus Christ not to have died a physical death upon the cross of Calvary.[157]

For Strobel, the search for the truth about Jesus Christ's death and resurrection did not end there. His continued inquiry went something like this: "Was Jesus' body placed in a tomb? Was the tomb found empty on the third day? And following His reported resurrection, to whom did Jesus first appear?" Lastly, Strobel's investigation considered the circumstantial evidence that existed, all of which gave credence to the very real possibility that something extraordinary had occurred. Following many in-depth discussions with prominent experts in the field of biblical research—including William Lane Craig, Gary Habermas, and J. P. Moreland—Strobel did the painstaking work of putting the pieces together. What follows is but a brief synopsis of some of the conclusions reached from his investigation.

Much of what Strobel concluded is based upon the available historical data, including the Christian creed (Nicene Creed, 325 AD) and the Gospels (Matthew, Mark, Luke, and John, 66–110 AD), all of which are considered to be valid sources of information. It stands to reason that it would be a daunting task to determine timelines for events from antiquity, and that biblical scholars might differ in their determination as to when the Gospels had been written. It is believed that the four canonical gospels were written within the following timeframes: Mark 66–70 AD, Matthew and Luke 85–90 AD, and John 90–110 AD.[158] In consideration that Christ's crucifixion and resurrection is dated as approximately 33 AD, it is conceivable that the Gospels could have well been the authors' firsthand accounts of Jesus' crucifixion.

Regardless, those who have seriously studied the historical significance of the Gospels believe they all had been written within a timeframe that speaks to their authenticity. Also, it is important to understand that the written word not only served as a historical record but was the primary means by which new information was shared during ancient times; therefore, the scribes were especially diligent in providing for absolute accuracy within their text.

The most extraordinary evidence of Jesus' death and resurrection remains the fearless manner in which His apostles continued to preach the good news following the crucifixion. Regardless how unpopular their message was in the eyes of the authorities, the apostles continued to fearlessly and relentlessly preach of Jesus' life and resurrection, even though doing so led to their own torturous deaths. It is highly doubtful the apostles would have endured all they did—knowing full well the consequences (Matthew 10:22; Luke 6:22; 10:29–30; John 15:18–25)—unless they believed in their body, mind, and soul that what they preached was true.

Discrepancies in the Gospels?

Critics often refer to the discrepancies in the gospels as proof that they are untrue. One example of a secondary discrepancy within the Gospels is the differing descriptions of the number and names of the women who found the empty tomb. On the contrary, Bible scholars conclude that the secondary discrepancies within the Gospels lend even more proof of their credibility. While the secondary information in the Gospels may differ, the core of the gospel stories remains consistent with one another. According to historians this fact adds to the credibility of the Gospels in that it proves the absence of plagiarism and is consistent with the way in which individuals report events from their own unique perspective.

Another aspect of the Easter story that at first glance might seem to discredit it, but ends up giving it more authenticity, relates to casting. For instance, if one were going to make up a story of this nature in ancient times, he would not have cast Joseph of Arimathea, a member of the Sanhedrin (a council of the Jewish court system), as the donor of Jesus' tomb. Why, you may ask? This is so because the Sanhedrin was the very council that had delivered Jesus for execution. Nor would a writer in that male-dominated society have cast lowly women as the first ones to discover Jesus' empty tomb. If this had merely been a work of fiction, the writers would have done everything in their power to conform to the cultural prejudices of the day in order to make their story more believable. They did not, and the story thus sounds way too much like life, not to be true.

The Bible relates that a great number of Jesus' followers had seen Him alive and well after His tomb was found to be empty. According to Scripture, the sightings of Jesus were not of an ethereal nature but involved various intimate encounters such as eating with Him, touching Him, and speaking with Him. Just as Jesus had fulfilled all the messianic prophecies concerning His life, death, and resurrection, so He also fulfilled the orthodox Jewish belief that following the Messiah's coming humankind's resurrection would be physical as well as spiritual in nature.

Given how the many pieces of the Easter story fit together so convincingly, one would be remiss not to conclude that Jesus was indeed crucified, that He died on the cross, that His tomb was found empty, that He was resurrected from the dead, and that life exists beyond the grave. This was Lee Strobel's conclusion as well, and like so many others with the courage to seek out God, this man began his search a skeptic and ended it a believer.[159]

Circumstantial Evidence

The circumstantial evidence of Jesus' life, crucifixion, and resurrection is as compelling a reason to believe as is the immediate aftermath of the Easter story. From the very beginning, Jesus' presence in the world changed lives—the lives of His disciples and the lives of skeptics, including Jesus' brother James and of course Paul of Tarsus. Amazingly, all of His followers were willing to die for the truth they found in Him. Many devout Jewish people's lives were changed; after centuries of protecting their monolithic religion and refusing to assimilate to the ways of their oppressors, many chose to follow Jesus. In so recognizing the triune God—one God in three Persons—rather than abiding by the strict interpretation of their monotheistic theology, they henceforth lived their lives through God's grace rather than through the law.[160] Out of this dramatic shift from law to grace emerged the Christian church, which swiftly swept the world and to this day remains strong with proselytes from all ethnic backgrounds and religions.

How Then Should We Live—and Die?

The implications of Jesus' death on the cross are literally never-ending. Through the power of God, Jesus was resurrected from the dead and given a place at the right hand of God the Father. Because our sins died in Christ, humankind was also given the promise of everlasting life through Jesus' sacrificial death and resurrection.

Not only does this amazing fact put a whole different face upon death itself, it does much the same for life as we know it within this earthly realm. I read through many illuminating books in preparation for writing this book, but it was a quote from the Russian writer Leo Tolstoy (of *War and Peace* fame) cited in Dr. Keller's masterpiece *The Reason for God* that best captured the essence of the impact that Christ's resurrection has had, not only in death but in living as well:

> My question—that which at the age of fifty brought me to the verge of suicide—was the simplest of questions, lying in the soul of every man . . . a question without an answer to which one cannot live. It was: "What will come of what I am doing today or tomorrow? What will come of my whole life? Why should I live, why wish for anything, or do anything?" It can also be expressed thus: Is there any meaning in my life that the inevitable death awaiting me does not destroy? [161]

Christ's answer to Tolstoy's question is a resounding *yes!* In fact, Christ's resurrection remains the only satisfactory answer available to any of us. Through Him, our lives are given tremendous meaning as we all are given a mission in this life. Each mission, whether we live our lives quietly loving and nurturing our families or are applauded by many through our efforts in humanitarian affairs worldwide, is of consequence to our heavenly Father. We are here not to waste our lives but to refine whatever gifts we have been blessed with and then to share those gifts in God's name. Will we make mistakes in this life? Yes indeed, both small mistakes as well as some whoppers. Will He deny us for our folly? Only if we deny Him!

Regardless of our talents or our mission, we are all expected to seek out God through every avenue available to us, in preparation for the day in which we return to Him. If we succeed in life in the way God intended, we will die unafraid, full of Him, wise in Him, and spent in Him.

Afterword

My hope is that after reading this book, it is clear to you that the one true God does not compartmentalize anything. God is not exclusive to any one area of life, for He created everything, and His handprint is found within all aspects of this life and the next. As such, neither personal prejudice nor popular social ideology can erase God from that which He alone has created.

Another aspect of God is that He is relational—and, having been created in God's own image, we were meant to be relational as well. As such, all of God's creation, beginning with its smallest parts, was meant to interact as a whole, whether that whole is a community, the human organism, or the entire universe. We can apply this premise to both God's visible and invisible world. As discussed in Chapter 6, neither God's visible nor His invisible world operate in a vacuum; rather, the two are in a state of constant interaction with one another.

Everything in life is in relationship with everything else, as well as with God. Even life's most unlikely opposites share a deep connection with each other. Have you ever noticed how God in His infinite wisdom more often than not attempts to teach us life's hardest lessons through the connection between apparent opposites? For instance, one cannot recognize goodness without knowing evil nor experience death without a life—or life without a death. So often our limited understanding gets in our way, and we resort to defensive compartmentalizing of everything in our lives, including God. With wave after wave of new data and situations bombarding us daily, we trick ourselves into believing that compartmentalization is our only recourse. God cautions us not to rely on our own understanding, and implores us to seek Him out before our lives begin to get messy, as they surely will.

Though a life of faith does not promise us a rose garden, it does provide us with that peace that passes all understanding as a consequence of knowing that God is with us in all things, from birth to death and beyond. Besides the number of hairs upon our heads, He knows intimately all the microscopic parts of each and every one of us. The Bible assures us that we humans are God's primary focus, and He wants us to make Him alone our primary focus as well.

I would encourage you to do your own personal investigation into where God figures in this life. Your search will take you in directions you might have never imagined. Today, as in no other time in human history, you will find God's handprint in both the seen and unseen world. There is no hyperbole in saying that such a search promises to be the journey of a lifetime—an endless journey that will change everything in your life and in the lives of those you touch.

Your quest for faith may begin in a book, though bear in mind that faith in God is more than a cognitive exercise. Faith, like love, requires practice. We cannot expect to fully know God by reading a book, or by merely giving Him lip service on Sunday mornings. Rather, we all need to work on a relationship with God throughout each week and throughout our whole lives. This is what our relational God requires of us and what we need to be about if we are going to begin experiencing His presence in all avenues of our lives. Though He shares both our joys and our sorrows even if we do not invite Him in, the truth is, when we face losing a loved one to death or face our own imminent demise, nothing helps more than to recognize that the one true God, who loves each of us beyond measure, is right by our side. And finally, when this life comes to an end and you open your eyes beyond the veil, then and only then will everything make perfect sense.

Appendix

Helpful Bible Verses Pertaining to Death and God's Grace

And I am convinced that nothing can ever separate us from God's love. Neither death nor life, neither angels nor demons, neither our fears for today nor our worries about tomorrow—not even the powers of hell can separate us from God's love. No power in the sky above or in the earth below—indeed, nothing in all creation will ever be able to separate us from the love of God that is revealed in Christ Jesus our Lord. (Romans 8:38–39)

For our dying bodies must be transformed into bodies that will never die; our mortal bodies must be transformed into immortal bodies. Then, when our dying bodies have been transformed into bodies that will never die, this Scripture will be fulfilled: "Death is swallowed up in victory. O death, where is your victory? O death, where is your sting?" (1 Corinthians 15:53–55)

Because God's children are human beings—made of flesh and blood—the Son also became flesh and blood. For only as a human being could he die, and only by dying could he break the power of the devil, who had the power of death. Only in this way could he set free all who have lived their lives as slaves to the fear of dying. (Hebrews 2:14–15)

I am the resurrection and the life. The one who believes in me will live, even though they die; and whoever lives by believing in me will never die. Do you believe this? (John 11:25–26, NIV)

I tell you the truth, anyone who obeys my teaching will never die! (John 8:51)

No longer will babies die when only a few days old. No longer will adults die before they have lived a full life. No longer will people be considered old at one hundred! Only the cursed will die that young! (Isaiah 65:20)

And now, dear brothers and sisters, we want you to know what will happen to the believers who have died so you will not grieve like people who have no hope. For since we believe that Jesus died and was raised to life again, we also believe that when Jesus returns, God will bring back believers who have died. (1 Thessalonians 4:13–14)

He will swallow up death forever! The Sovereign LORD will wipe away all tears. He will remove forever the insults and mockery against his land and people. The LORD has spoken! (Isaiah 25:8)

It is the same way with the resurrection of the dead. Our earthly bodies are planted in the ground when we die, but they will be raised to live forever. Our bodies are buried in brokenness, but they will be raised in glory. They are buried in weakness, but they will be raised in strength. They are buried as natural human bodies, but they will be raised as spiritual bodies. For as there are natural bodies, there are also spiritual bodies. (1 Corinthians 15:42–44)

Yes, we are fully confident, and we would rather be away from these earthly bodies, for then we will be at home with the Lord. (2 Corinthians 5:8)

So you see, just as death came into the world through a man, now the resurrection from the dead has begun through another man. Just as everyone dies because we all belong to Adam, everyone who belongs to Christ will be given new life. But there is an order to this resurrection: Christ was raised as the first of the harvest; then all who belong to Christ will be raised when he comes back. (1 Corinthians 15:21–23)

For our present troubles are small and won't last very long. Yet they produce for us a glory that vastly outweighs them and will last forever! So we don't look at the troubles we can see now; rather, we fix our gaze on things that cannot be seen. For the things we see now will soon be gone, but the things we cannot see will last forever. (2 Corinthians 4:17–18)

He will wipe every tear from their eyes, and there will be no more death or sorrow or crying or pain. All these things are gone forever. (Revelation 21:4)

God blesses those who mourn, for they will be comforted. (Matthew 5:4)

Don't let your hearts be troubled. Trust in God, and trust also in me. There is more than enough room in my Father's home. If this were not so, would I have told you that I am going to prepare a place for you? (John 14:1–2)

All praise to God, the Father of our Lord Jesus Christ. God is our merciful Father and the source of all comfort. He comforts us in all our troubles so that we can comfort others. When they are troubled, we will be able to give them the same comfort God has given us. (2 Corinthians 1:3–4)

Do not be afraid, for I have redeemed you. I have called you by name; you are mine. When you go through deep waters, I will be with you. When you go through the rivers of difficulty, you will not drown. When you walk through the fire of oppression, you will not be burned up; the flames will not consume you. (Isaiah 43:1–2)

So do not fear, for I am with you; do not be dismayed, for I am your God. I will strengthen you and help you; I will uphold you with my righteous right hand. (Isaiah 41:10, NIV)

God is our refuge and strength, always ready to help in times of trouble. So we will not fear when earthquakes come and the mountains crumble into the sea. (Psalm 46:1–2)

Your promise revives me; it comforts me in all my troubles. (Psalm 119:50)

The LORD is my rock, my fortress, and my savior; my god is my rock, in whom I find protection. He is my shield, the power that saves me, and my place of safety. I called on the LORD, who is worthy of praise, and he saved me from my enemies. (Psalm 18:2–3)

So humble yourselves under the mighty power of God, and at the right time he will lift you up in honor. Give all your worries and cares to God, for he cares about you. (1 Peter 5:6–7)

I will never leave you. I will never abandon you. (Hebrews 13:5)

Don't worry about anything; instead, pray about everything. Tell God what you need, and thank him for all he has done. Then you will experience God's peace, which exceeds anything we can understand. His peace will guard your hearts and minds as you live in Christ Jesus. (Philippians 4:6–7)

For we died and were buried with Christ by baptism. And just as Christ was raised from the dead by the glorious power of the Father, now we also may live new lives. (Romans 6:4)

But we are citizens of heaven, where the Lord Jesus Christ lives. And we are eagerly waiting for him to return as our Savior. He will take our weak mortal bodies and change them into glorious bodies like his own, using the same power with which he will bring everything under his control. (Philippians 3:20–21)

The LORD is close to the brokenhearted; he rescues those whose spirits are crushed. The righteous person faces many troubles, but the LORD comes to the rescue each time. For the LORD protects the bones of the righteous; not one of them is broken! (Psalm 34:18–20)

Our God is a God who saves! The Sovereign LORD rescues us from death. (Psalm 68:20)

For God so loved the world that he gave his one and only Son, that whoever believes in him shall not perish but have eternal life. (John 3:16)

For the wages of sin is death, but the gift of God is eternal life through Christ Jesus our Lord. (Romans 6:23, NIV)

And now he has made all of this plain to us by the appearing of Christ Jesus, our Savior. He broke the power of death and illuminated the way to life and immortality through the Good News. (2 Timothy 1:10)

But for me, God will redeem my life. He will snatch me from the grave. (Psalm 49:15)

And I assure you that the time is coming, indeed it's here now, when the dead will hear my voice—the voice of the Son of God. And those who listen will live. (John 5:25)

For when we died with Christ we were set free from the power of sin. And since we died with Christ, we know we will also live with him. We are sure of this because Christ was raised from the dead, and He will never die again. Death no longer has any power over Him. (Romans 6:7–9)

And I heard a voice from heaven saying, "Write this down: Blessed are those who die in the Lord from now on. Yes, says the Spirit, they are blessed indeed, for they will rest from their hard work; for their good deeds follow them!" (Revelation 14:13)

The young women will dance for joy, and the men—old and young—will join in the celebration. I will turn their morning into joy. I will comfort them and exchange their sorrow for rejoicing. (Jeremiah 31:13)

What is the price of two sparrows—one copper coin? But not a single sparrow can fall to the ground without your Father knowing it. (Matthew 10:29)

Even when I walk through the darkest valley, I will not be afraid, for you are close beside me. Your rod and your staff comfort me. You prepare a feast for me in the presence of my enemies. You honor me by anointing my head with oil. My cup overflows with blessings. Surely your goodness and unfailing love will pursue me all the days of my life, and I will live in the house of the LORD forever. (Psalm 23:4–6)

For the mountains may move and the hills disappear, but even then my faithful love for you will remain. My covenant of blessings will never be broken," says the LORD, who has mercy on you. (Isaiah 54:10)

For the LORD your God is living among you. He is a mighty savior. He will take delight in you with gladness. With his love, he will calm all your fears. He will rejoice over you with joyful songs. (Zephaniah 3:17)

The LORD keeps you from all harm and watches over your life. The LORD keeps watch over you as you come and go, both now and forever. (Psalm 121:7–8)

He heals the brokenhearted and bandages their wounds. (Psalm 147:3)

For that is what God is like. He is our God forever and ever, and he will guide us until we die. (Psalm 48:14)

You have allowed me to suffer much hardship, but you will restore me to life again and lift me up to even greater honor and comfort once again. (Psalm 71:20–21)

Have you never heard? Have you never understood? The Lord is the everlasting God, the Creator of all the earth. He never grows weak or weary. No one can measure the depths of his understanding. He gives power to the weak and strength to the powerless. (Isaiah 40:28–29)

Trust in the Lord with all your heart; do not depend on your own understanding. Seek his will in all you do, and he will show you which path to take. (Proverbs 3:5–6)

The Lord is righteous in everything he does; he is filled with kindness. The Lord is close to all who call on him, yes, to all who call on him in truth. He grants the desires of those who fear him; he hears their cries for help and rescues them. (Psalm 145:17–19)

For you are my hiding place; you protect me from trouble. You surround me with songs of victory. The Lord says, "I will guide you along the best pathway for your life. I will advise you and watch over you." (Psalm 32:7–8)

And we know that God causes everything to work together for the good of those who love God and are called according to his purpose for them. For God knew his people in advance, and he chose them to become like his Son, so that his Son would be the firstborn among many brothers and sisters. And having chosen them, he called them to come to him. And having called them, he gave them right standing with himself. And having given them right standing, he gave them his glory. (Romans 8:28–30)

So be strong and courageous! Do not be afraid and do not panic before them. For the LORD your God will personally go ahead of you. He will neither fail you nor abandon you. (Deuteronomy 31:6)

For God made Christ, who never sinned, to be the offering for our sin, so that we could be made right with God through Christ. (2 Corinthians 5:21)

Give your burdens to the LORD, and he will take care of you. He will not permit the godly to slip and fall. (Psalm 55:22)

Then call on me when you are in trouble, and I will rescue you, and you will give me glory. (Psalm 50:15)

Come close to God, and God will come close to you. (James 4:8)

Yes, and the Lord will deliver me from every evil attack and will bring me safely into his heavenly Kingdom. All glory to God forever and ever! (2 Timothy 4:18)

Jesus responded, "Didn't I tell you that you would see God's glory if you believe?" (John 11:40)

So don't be afraid, little flock. For it gives your Father great happiness to give you the Kingdom. (Luke 12:32)

Those who are victorious will sit with me on my throne, just as I was victorious and sat with my Father on his throne. (Revelation 3:21)

So also Christ was offered once for all time as a sacrifice to take away the sins of many people. He will come again, not to deal with our sins, but to bring salvation to all who are eagerly waiting for him. (Hebrews 9:28)

Some of you were once like that. But you were cleansed; you were made holy; you were made right with God by calling on the name of the Lord Jesus Christ and by the Spirit of our God. (1 Corinthians 6:11)

You were dead because of your sins and because your sinful nature was not yet cut away. Then God made you alive with Christ, for he forgave all our sins. He canceled the record of the charges against us and took it away by nailing it to the cross. (Colossians 2:13–14)

So now there is no condemnation for those who belong to Christ Jesus. And because you belong to him, the power of the life-giving Spirit has freed you from the power of sin that leads to death. (Romans 8:1–2)

For the angel of the LORD is a guard; he surrounds and defends all who fear him. (Psalm 34:7)

But you are not like that, for the Holy One has given you his Spirit, and all of you know the truth. (1 John 2:20)

But if we are living in the light, as God is in the light, then we have fellowship with each other, and the blood of Jesus, his Son, cleanses us from all sin. (1 John 1:7)

And God will raise us from the dead by his power, just as he raised our Lord from the dead. (1 Corinthians 6:14)

I prayed to the LORD and he answered me. He freed me from all my fears. (Psalm 34:4)

For God bought you with a high price. So you must honor God with your body. (1 Corinthians 6:20)

Jesus personally carried our sins in his body on the cross so that we can be dead to sin and live for what is right. By his wounds you are healed. Once you were like sheep who wandered away. But now you have turned to your Shepherd, the Guardian of your souls. (1 Peter 2:24–25)

When he died, he died once to break the power of sin. But now that he lives, he lives for the glory of God. So you also should consider yourselves to be dead to the power of sin and alive to God through Christ Jesus. (Romans 6:10–11)

All who are victorious will be clothed in white. I will never erase their names from the Book of Life, but I will announce before my Father and his angels that they are mine. (Revelation 3:5)

Endnotes

Chapter 1—"I Love You," Truly

1. Robert Taibbi, "Narcissist or Just Self-Centered? 4 Ways to Tell," *Psychology Today*, September 23, 2015, https://www.psychologytoday.com/us/blog/fixing-families/201509/narcissist-or-just-self-centered-4-ways-tell (accessed June 30, 2019).

2. Neal Burton, "These Are the 7 Types of Love," *Psychology Today*, June 25, 2016, https://www.psychologytoday.com/us/blog/hide-and-seek/201606/these-are-the-7-types-love (accessed June 30, 2019).

3. Jack Zavada, "4 Types of Love in the Bible," Learn Religions, May 6, 2019, https://www.learnreligions.com/types-of-love-in-the-bible-700177 (accessed June 30, 2019).

4. Erich Fromm, *The Art of Loving* (New York: Harper & Row, 2006), 19.

5. Ibid., 23.

6. Ibid., 5.

7. Ibid., 24, 116.

8. Ibid., 115–116.

9. "Corrie Ten Boom Quotes," Brainy Quote, https://www.brainyquote.com/quotes/corrie_ten_boom_381184.

Chapter 3—Who Has It Right?

10. James M. Rochford, *Too Good To Be True?: How We Get to Heaven, What It Will Be Like, and Why We Can't Live without It* (Columbus, OH: New Paradigm Publishing, 2016), 7.

11. "Religion," *Wikipedia*, https://en.wikipedia.org/wiki/Religion (accessed June 30, 2019).

12. See, for example, Bhikkhu Bodhi, *The Eightfold Path, Way to the End of Suffering* (Onalaska, WA: BPS Pariyatti Publishing, 2008), 11.

13. Harold Coward, ed., *Life after Death in World Religions* (Maryknoll, NY: Orbis, 1997), 90.

14. "History of Buddhism In India," Wikipedia, https://en.wikipedia.org/wiki/History_of_Buddhism_in_India (accessed June 30, 2019).

15. "Religion," *Wikipedia*.

16. Sebastian Saenz, "How the Major Religions View the Afterlife," Gale Encyclopedia of the Unusual and Unexplained, https://www.encyclopedia.com/science/encyclopedias-almanacs-transcripts-and-maps/how-major-religions-view-afterlife (accessed May 11, 2020).

17. Douglas R. Groothuis, *Unmasking the New Age* (Downers Grove, IL: IVP Books, 1986), 18, 20.

18. Phil Mason, *Quantum Glory: The Science of Heaven Invading Earth* (Maricopa, AZ: New Earth Tribe Publications, 2010), 36.

19. Coward, *Life after Death in World Religions,* 19.

20. Neal Gillman, *The Death of Death: Resurrection and Immortality in Jewish Thought* (Woodstock, VT: Jewish Lights, 1997), 196–214.

21. Vexen Crabtree, "Hebrew Scriptures and Christian Holy Bibles across Different Traditions," The Human Truth Foundation (2012), http://www.holybooks.info/bible.html (accessed June 30, 2019).

22. "Comparison Table between Christianity, Islam and Judaism," Christianity in View, http://christianityinview.com/xncomparison.html (accessed June 30, 2019).

23. Coward, *Life after Death in World Religions,* 48.

24. "Survey: 32% of Atheists & Agnostics Believe in an Afterlife," The Skeptics Guide to the Universe, https://legacy.theskepticsguide.org/one-third-of-atheists-agnostics-believe-in-an-afterlife (accessed May 11, 2020).

25. "Religion," *Wikipedia*.

26. Timothy Keller, *The Reason for God* (New York: Penguin Group Inc., 2009), 16.

27. Sheldon Vanauken. *A Severe Mercy* (New York: Harper & Row, Publishers, Inc., 1979), 89–90.

Chapter 4—The Process of Dying

28. Andre Klarsfeld and Frederic Revah, *The Biology of Death: Origins of Mortality* (Ithaca, NY: Cornell University Press, 2003), 182.

29. Sam Parnia, *Erasing Death* (New York: HarperCollins, 2014), 24.

30. Sam Parnia, *What Happens When We Die?: A Groundbreaking Study into the Nature of Life and Death* (Carlsbad, CA: Hay House, 2006), 36.

31. American Red Cross, *Responding to Emergencies: Comprehensive First Aid/CPR/AED* (Yardley, PA: The StayWell Company, 2017).

32. Parnia, *What Happens When We Die?*, 88.

33. Ross Pomeroy, "Why We Should Harvest Blood from the Dead," *RealClear Science*, July 22, 2015, https://www.realclearscience.com/blog/2015/07/a_simple_solution_to_end_blood_shortages.html (accessed May 11, 2020).

34. Parnia, *Erasing Death*, 49.

35. American Heart Association, "Heart Disease and Stroke Statistics 2017 At-a-Glance," https://healthmetrics.heart.org/wp-content/uploads/2017/06/Heart-Disease-and-Stroke-Statistics-2017-ucm_491265.pdf (accessed June 30, 2019).

36. Samuel French, *Death Takes a Holiday*, fifth edition (Binghamton, NY: Vail-Ballou Press, 1935), 50.

Chapter 5—From Death and Back

37. David San Filippo, "Religious Interpretations of Near-Death Experiences," https://www.near-death.com/science/articles/religious-interpretations-of-ndes.html (accessed June 30, 2019).

38. Ibid.

39. "Near-Death Studies, Research—History and background," Wikipedia, https://en.wikipedia.org/wiki/Near-death_studies (accessed June 30, 2019).

40. Janice Miner Holden, Bruce Greyson, and Debbie James, eds. *The Handbook of Near-Death Experiences: Thirty Years of Investigation* (Santa Barbara, CA: ABC-CLIO, 2009), 6.

41. "Near-Death Studies, Research—History and Background."

42. Ibid.

43. Jeffrey Long, *Evidence of the Afterlife: The Science of Near-Death Experiences* (New York: HarperCollins, 2011), Introduction, 1–19.

44. "Key Facts about Near-Death Experiences," International Association for Near Death Studies, August 29, 2017, https://iands.org/ndes/about-ndes/key-nde-facts21.html?showall=1 (accessed June 30, 2019).

45. Long, *Evidence of the Afterlife,* 177–178.

46. Holden, Greyson, and James, *Handbook of Near-Death Experiences,* 42–43.

47. Ibid., 56.

48. "Distressing Near-Death Experiences," International Association for Near Death Studies, December 14, 2017, https://iands.org/ndes/about-ndes/distressing-ndes.html (accessed June 30, 2019).

49. Jeffrey Long, *God and the Afterlife,* (New York: HarperCollins Publisher, 2016), 161.

50. Howard Storm, *My Descent into Death: A Second Chance at Life* (New York: Random House, 2005), 10-18.

51. Holden, Greyson, and James, *Handbook of Near-Death Experiences,* 182.

52. J. Isamu Yamamoto, "The Near Death Experience" (Part Two), Christian Research Institute, June 10, 2009, https://www.equip.org/article/the-near-death-experience-part-two (accessed June 30, 2019).

53. Ibid.

54. Storm, *My Descent into Death*, 73.

55. San Filippo, "Religious Interpretations of Near-Death Experiences."

56. Eben Alexander, *Proof of Heaven: A Neurosurgeon's Journey into the Afterlife* (New York: Simon and Schuster, 2012), 141–142.

57. Ibid., 142–143.

58. Long, *God and the Afterlife*, 69.

Chapter 6—The Omniscient God

59. "Physics: Newtonian Physics," Encyclopedia.com, last updated March 18, 2020, https://www.encyclopedia.com/science/science-magazines/physics-newtonian-physics.

60. "What's the Difference between Materialism and Naturalism?" International Skeptics Forum, http://www.internationalskeptics.com/forums/showthread.php?t=9386 (accessed June 30, 2019).

61. Grant R. Jeffrey, *The Signature of God*, revised edition (Colorado Springs: WaterBrook, 2010), 106.

62. Sarah A. McGee, *Heaven's Reality: Lifting the Quantum Veil* (Denver: Glistening Prospect Bookhouse, 2016), 21.

63. Mason, *Quantum Glory*, 56.

64. Ibid.

65. Ibid., 62.

66. Ibid., 35.

67. Ibid., 83.

68. Ibid., 87.

69. Ibid., 86.

70. Ibid., 83.

71. McGee, *Heaven's Reality*, 83.

Chapter 7—Miracles, Great and Small

72. As quoted by Eric Metaxas, *Miracles: What They Are, Why They Happen, and How They Can Change Your Life* (New York: Penguin, 2014), 11.

73. Ibid.

74. Kenneth L. Woodward, *The Book of Miracles* (New York: Touchstone, 2000), 39.

75. Ibid., 136.

76. Ibid., 173.

77. Ibid., 184-185.

78. David L. Weddle, *Miracles: Wonder and Meaning in World Religions* (New York: New York University Press, 2010), 69, 140.

79. Ibid.

80. John Weldon, "A Contrast between Biblical Christianity and New Age or Spiritistic Theology and Philosophy," The John Ankerberg Show (2005), https://www.jashow.org/articles/a-contrast-between-biblical-christianity-and-new-age-or-spiritistic-theology-and-philosophy (accessed June 30, 2019).

81. Woodward, *Book of Miracles*, 21.

82. Ibid.

83. McGee, *Heaven's Reality*, 151.

84. Mason, *Quantum Glory*, 115.

85. Ibid., 237.

86. Ibid., 238.

87. Ibid., 239.

88. Ibid., pp. 238–239.

89. "World Population," Wikipedia, https://en.wikipedia.org/wiki/World_population (accessed June 30, 2019).

90. Mason, *Quantum Glory*, 187.

91. Karin Lehnardt, "90 Amazing Human Body Facts," Fact Retriever, https://www.factretriever.com/body-facts (accessed June 30, 2019).

92. Kate Ng, "18 Facts You Didn't Know about How Amazing Your Body Is," *Independent,* https://www.independent.com.uk/life-style/health-and-families/features/18-facts-you-didn't-know-about-how-amazing-your-body-is-a6725486.html (accessed June 30, 2019).

93. Metaxas, *Miracles,* 36–45, 48–56.

94. Grant R. Jeffrey, *Creation: Remarkable Evidence of God's Design* (Colorado Springs: WaterBrook, 2003), 88–89.

95. Metaxas, *Miracles,* 38.

96. Ibid., 39–40.

97. Ibid., 40.

98. Ibid., 41.

99. Ibid., 40–41.

100. "Origin of Water on Earth," *Wikipedia,* https://en.wikipedia.org/wiki/Origin_of_water_on_Earth (accessed June 30, 2019).

101. Metaxas, *Miracles,* 42–43.

102. David Biello, "The Origin of Oxygen in Earth's Atmosphere," *Scientific American,* August 19, 2009, https://www.scientificamerican.com/article/origin-of-oxygen-in-atmosphere (accessed March 26, 2020).

103. Metaxas, *Miracles,* 27, 48.

104. Quoted in Ibid., 33.

Chapter 8—The Infallible Word

105. "How Many Bibles Are Sold Each Year?" The Bible Answer, https://thebibleanswer.org/bibles-sold-each-year (accessed May 11, 2020).

106. Paul Enns, *The Moody Handbook of Theology* (Chicago: Moody, 2008), 372, 377.

107. "What Happens after Death?" Bibleinfo, http://www.bibleinfo.com/en/questions/what-does-bible-say-about-death (accessed June 30, 2019).

108. Enns, *Moody Handbook of Theology,* 378.

109. "Does the Bible Say Anything about Near-Death Experiences?" CompellingTruth.org, https://www.compellingtruth.org/near-death-experiences.html (accessed June 30, 2019).

110. John W. Price, *Revealing Heaven* (New York: Harper One, 2013), 37, 40, 43.

111. Ibid., 144.

112. John Burke, *Imagine Heaven* (Grand Rapids, MI: Baker, 2015), 174.

113. Long, *God and the Afterlife*, 69.

114. Jeffrey, *The Signature of God*, 127.

115. Ibid., 132, 133, 152–153.

116. Ibid., 67–69, 175–176.

117. Ibid., 63–64.

118. Ibid., 69.

119. Ibid., 56.

120. Michael Guillen, *Amazing Truths: How Science and the Bible Agree* (Grand Rapids, MI: Zondervan, 2015), 89–91.

121. Jeffrey, *The Signature of God*, 107.

122. John Polkinghorne, *Quantum Physics and Theology: An Unexpected Kinship* (London: Society for Promoting Christian Knowledge, 2007), 55.

123. Guillen, *Amazing Truths*, 34.

124. Ibid., 60, 105.

125. Ibid., 110.

126. Ibid., 69.

Chapter 9—Our Father

127. Guillen, *Amazing Truths*, 162.

128. Lita Cosner, "How Does the Bible Teach 6,000 Years?" *Creation*, Vol 35, No. 1 (January 2013): 54–55.

129. Arunodhayan Sam Solomon F., Melwin, Banu, Sashikala, "Superiority of the Human Brain over the Computer World in Terms of Memory, Network, Retrieval, and Processing," *American Journal of Engineering Research*, Volume 3, Issue 5 (2014): 230–239.

130. Guillen, *Amazing Truths*, 162-163.

131. Ibid., 146-147.

132. Ibid., 75–76.

133. Ibid., 76, 80

Chapter 10—Full Circle

134. Guillen, *Amazing Truths*, 146.

135. Elizabeth Kubler-Ross, *On Death and Dying* (New York: Macmillan Publishing Co., Inc., 1978) 38–137.

136. Mark Connelly, "Kubler-Ross Five Stage Model," August 30, 2018, https://www.change-management-coach.com/kubler-ross.html (accessed June 30, 2019).

137. Kubler-Ross, *On Death and Dying*, 5, 14.

138. Ibid., 11.

139. Ibid., 15.

140. M. Dadfar and D. Lester, "Religiously, Spirituality and Death Anxiety," *Austin Journal of Psychiatry and Behavioral Sciences*, Volume 4, Issue 1 (2017): 1061.

141. Kubler-Ross, *On Death and Dying*, 14.

142. "Suicide," The National Institute of Mental Health, https://www.nimh.nih.gov/health/statistics/suicide.shtml (accessed June 30, 2019).

143. E. Rupert Kenneth, *Empathy, Love and Life beyond Self* (N.a: The Vita-Copia Group, 2014), 4.

Chapter 11—It's Your Choice

144. Todd M. Johnson, "Christianity Is Fragmented—Why?" Gordon-Conwell Theological Seminary, https://www.gordonconwell.edu/blog/christianity-is-fragmented-why (accessed May 11, 2020).

145. C. S. Lewis, *Mere Christianity*, 54.

146. "List of Christian Denominations by Number of Members," Wikipedia, https://en.wikipedia.org/wiki/List_of_Christian_denominations_by_number_of_members (accessed June 30, 2019).

147. Jeffrey, *The Signature of God*, 13.

148. Keller, *The Reason for God*, 12–13, 16.

149. Ibid., 26–27.

150. "Christian Humanitarian Aid," Wikipedia, https://en.wikipedia.org/wiki/Christian_humanitarian_aid (accessed June 30, 2019).

151. Keller, *The Reason for God*, 65–68.

152. Henry M. Morris, "Bible-Believing Scientists of the Past," Institute for Creation Research, January 1, 1982, https://www.icr.org/article/bible-believing-scientists-past (accessed June 30, 2019).

153. John C. Lennox, *Can Science Explain Everything?* (Epsom: The Good Book Company, 2019), 12.

154. Guillen, *Amazing Truths*, 110.

Chapter 12—It Is Finished!

155. Timothy Keller, *Jesus the King* (New York: Penguin Books, 2016), 247.

156. Lee Strobel, *The Case for Christ* (Grand Rapids, MI: Zondervan, 1998), 193.

157. Ibid., 193–204.

158. "Gospel," *Wikipedia*, https://en.wikipedia.org/wiki/gospel.

159. Strobel, *Case for Christ*, 205–243.

160. Ibid., 246–250.

161. Leo Tolstoy, *A Confession*; quoted in Keller, *The Reason for God*, 209.